BRITAIN IN OLD PHOTOGRAPHS

NORTHALLERTON

MICHAEL RIORDAN

SUTTON PUBLISHING LIMITED

Sutton Publishing Limited
Phoenix Mill · Thrupp · Stroud
Gloucestershire · GL5 2BU

First published 1996

Copyright © Michael Riordan, 1996

Cover photographs: *front*: Wright's
Confectioner's, 1910; *back*: the Gardner
family in 1911.

British Library Cataloguing in Publication Data
A catalogue record for this book is available from the
British Library.

ISBN 0-7509-0839-4

Typeset in 10/12 Perpetua.
Typesetting and origination by
Sutton Publishing Limited.
Printed in Great Britain by
Ebenezer Baylis, Worcester.

ACKNOWLEDGEMENTS

For the use of their photographs and essential help with identification and
interpretation:

Dorothy Alderson • Benny Archer, MBE • Ron Bateson • Derek Bell • Don Bell • Pat
and Geoff Blair • Peter Beadle • Harold Brown • Margaret Calvert • Joan and Barry
Cawthorne • M. Chapman • John Clapham , Paul Clarke • Elsie Coombes
J.R. ('Bobby') Cooper • Lou Dale • George Darwin • E. Dennis • John Farndale
Eileen Gaskell • Brian Glasper • D. Gibson • Ivy Hepplestone • Mr Johnson
George Kelley • Elma King • Chris Kirk • Katherine Lart • Pearl Lynas
Doreen Newcombe • Derek Parkin • Ernest Pearson • John Pearson • Joyce Render
Major George Riordan • David Robinson • Mark Rountree • Dorothy and Ken Sawyer
Dr David Severs • Brian Simpson • Miss Kathleen Sunley • Harry Thompson
Joan Wilbor • Maureen Willoughby • Ken Wilson • Dr Wyon • Dorothy Young

For the courtesy afforded and provision of reference facilities:

North Yorkshire Reference Library • Northallerton North Yorkshire County Record
Office • Northallerton Darlington Local History Library • York City Reference
Library • British Library, London • Christ Church College, Oxford.

CONTENTS

Sidney Weighell was born and educated in Northallerton, attending the East Road School, and rose to the very pinnacle of the national Trades Union tree, becoming the General Secretary (1975–83) and leader of the National Union of Railwaymen. This was an unprecedented achievement by a local person. William Weighell, his grandfather, and Tom Weighell, his father who gained the BEM and MBE, were both staunch railway trade unionists and Sid followed in their footsteps, becoming a local NUR official by the time he was twenty. Union duties took him away from professional football where he had played two seasons for Sunderland Reserves. Despite his success and national eminence, whether with the railways or in his hometown, Sid Weighell has always remained 'a man of the people'.

INTRODUCTION

E ven in 1739 Roger Gale of Scruton, Northallerton's first historian, called Northallerton an 'ancient town'. He stressed its Roman origins and the fact that it had been a thriving Saxon Borough with a stone church, sixty-six villeins (freemen) and jurisdiction over twenty-one surrounding places including Brunton (Brompton) and Romundebi (Romanby).

At the basis of Northallerton's prominence and future development were two salient factors: its central position in a rich alluvial agricultural area and its situation on the main eastern route from England to Scotland. The latter has profoundly influenced the town down the ages from as early as the English-Scottish wars which – raging for 300 years – included the 1138 Battle of the Standard fought with great Scottish losses three miles north of Northallerton; saw the burning of the church and town by the Scots in 1318 and brought successive English armies to the town with their kings – Edward I, Edward II and Edward III – who stayed at the 'Bishop's Palace' (now the cemetery site).

Later, because of its situation on the Great North Road between London and Edinburgh, the town played a major role in the stage-coach era (1770–1841). It became an important coaching centre with the Golden Lion, King's Head, Black Bull and Old Golden Lion receiving a plethora of coaches such as the 'Telegraph', 'Wellington' and 'Queen Charlotte'.

These colourful and exciting times came to an abrupt end with the opening of the Darlington–York railway on 30 March 1841. With the arrival of the 'Iron Horse', Northallerton's population was reduced but this was only temporary – 104 trains stopped each weekday in 1885 and by 1900 many railwaymen swelled the population. The town's nodal position had again proved crucial, giving Northallerton a permanent place on one of the main railway lines in the country.

Meanwhile, in more settled times, Northallerton had become renowned for its markets, held every Wednesday from before 1100, and four annual fairs granted in 1200, 1554, and 1609. The markets became the lynch-pin of the district's trade and economy, supplemented by the excellent fairs which drew praise from national observers such as William Camden (1586): 'Northallerton . . . which is nothing but a long street; yet the most throng Beast-fair upon St Bartholomew's day, that ever I saw.' This was the 'olde worlde' of Northallerton which was to be revolutionized by irrevocable changes and massive events during the period covered by these photographs.

The two world wars greatly affected Northallerton, with the sad loss of ninety-eight men in the First World War, not counting those who died later as a result of the conflict, or those wounded, maimed and gassed. Forty-one laid down their lives in the Second World War, nearly half of whom had only recently left Northallerton Grammar School. Also commemorated on the Northallerton war memorial are the crews of No. 6 Bomber Group Royal Canadian Air Force who flew from numerous nearby stations with enormous losses – at Leeming, for example, 903 gallant flyers were killed between 1943 and 1945.

Previously, titanic technological changes had been initiated at Northallerton by the introduction, in 1899, of both the motor car and urban electric lighting by John Ernest Hutton of Solberge Hall. He manufactured cars from 1900 for a time at his 'Ohm Electric Works' in north High Street. This was the commencement of an awe-inspiring revolution in industry, farming and other social aspects. Industry was electrified and mechanized and gradually concentrations of industrial organizations developed at the

North End and the Springwell Lane areas. Farming was slowly mechanized, this change being characterized by the demise of the horse in favour of the tractor. The motor car and other vehicles began to monopolize the roads and dominate the town.

Great improvements were made in education especially in the provision of new schools: the Applegarth Infants' School was completed in 1908; the reorganized Northallerton Grammar School was opened in 1909; the Allertonshire County Modern School was erected by 1941 and Mill Hill Primary School was built in 1956.

Probably the biggest social revolution in the town's modern history occurred in the spheres of sanitation, housing and health. In 1894 a reservoir was constructed at Oakdale near Osmotherly from which fresh water was piped to Northallerton, replacing its two hundred wells. The water supply was further improved over the years until the Sheepwash Reservoir was activated in 1953. A sewage plant was provided in 1898 which was also extended and refined gradually.

Over the centuries domestic housing had been confined to the High Street, this being changed when South Parade was developed (1860–1880) along with the Malpas Road district. Before and after the First World War, houses were built peripherally on the town approaches – Thirsk, Boroughbridge, Brompton and Crosby roads. But although twenty council houses were built at Vicar's Croft in the 1930s, over a third of the population lived in the dark, narrow yards.

More council houses were erected on the eastern side of the town in 1948 and finally a concentrated programme to demolish the yards and re-house the occupants in new council houses commenced in the mid-1950s. This process ended in the late 1960s, by which time there were 1,500 council houses and many new private housing developments which had appeared simultaneously.

Because of the amelioration of living conditions, health had improved dramatically since the nineteenth century. The Cottage Hospital, created in 1877 from Vine House and re-named the Rutson Hospital in 1905 after its benefactor, Henry Rutson of Newby Wiske, was a great boon.

A second hospital was one of the greatest assets ever to grace the town, coming via a wartime emergency hospital established in 1939 to deal with civilian bombing casualties; this became the Royal Air Force Hospital Northallerton from 1943 until 1947 and finally, in 1948, the Friarage Hospital. The latter has grown from small beginnings and prospered, serving a large catchment area and developing a widespread and deserved reputation for professional proficiency, allied to humanity, true hospitality and friendliness – the 'Friarage spirit'. With such a general hospital in a town of its size, Northallerton is indeed fortunate.

Another momentous event of vital importance to Northallerton was the siting of the North Riding County Hall headquarters on the old racecourse in 1903. In 1736 and 1785 North Riding buildings had established Northallerton as the county town which was confirmed by the building of the County Hall, followed by extensions in 1916, 1930 and 1940, as well as the erection of other substantial county buildings. This North Riding complex ensured that Northallerton became the county town of North Yorkshire in 1974.

There have been colossal changes in Northallerton and the town has mushroomed and developed almost beyond recognition. Yet in essence, has it changed that much? John Leland's description in 1538 was: 'The Towne of Northalverton is yn one fair long Streate lying by South and North'. The central focus is still on the High Street – the heart and pulse of the town. It is certain that every person featured in this volume knew it well – as will generations of people to come.

HISTORIC NORTHALLERTON

Castle Hills is the most ancient, controversial and enigmatic historical site in the Northallerton district. Historian Roger Gale (1739) believed a Roman military station had existed there and this is strongly borne out by the discovery of Roman remains such as urns and a multiplicity of coins. The number of finds culminated when the Great Northern Railway line was built in 1838; a well, a votive altar to the Roman V Legion (who entered England in 122 AD), a drainage system and further coins were discovered. This sketch of a towering Castle Hills was produced in the 1700s before it had been levelled in 1801, divided into fields in 1808 and finally almost being removed to construct the embankment for the railway over Northallerton in 1838/9. Down the centuries Castle Hills played host to numerous English armies, many led by royalty, and the question whether it was a natural phenomenon or man-made by the Romans or an even earlier race is still unsolved.

A 1925 postcard captures Northallerton Parish Church of All Saints, dominating as it had, for nearly a millennium, the town and the Great North Road from London to Edinburgh running through it. The great size of the church is attributable to its situation as a bishop's church – the Prince Bishops of Durham held it from 1086 to 1838. Saxon crosses and fragments from the eighth and ninth centuries have been found during church renovations, indicating the existence of a Saxon stone church, and Christian worship has thus taken place here for well over a thousand years.

Vicarages allied with Northallerton Parish Church have existed on this site since the 1200s and this particular vicarage was erected for the Revd George Townsend in 1828, he being famous for his ecumenical views which he put to the Pope in an audience with the latter at the Vatican. When a modern vicarage was built in the 1960s, Townsend's building was used by Northallerton Rural District Council and then the Hambleton District Council. It was demolished in 1988 to make way for a private housing development – Applegarth Court, which has retained the Latin inscription by George Townsend from the vicarage door as well as an 1828 firemark.

The Battle of the Standard is dramatically depicted here by Sir John Gilbert RA in 1893, depicting the English troops gathered round the Standard with the Bishop of Orkney, Ralph Newell, exhorting them to great deeds in the coming battle. The English were gathered by Archbishop Thurstan of York and opposed by a mixture of Scots commanded by their king, David, supported by his son Prince Henry. Standard Hill, three miles north of Northallerton, was the battleground, and in the hectic fray which occurred, in the early morning of 22 August 1138 the Scots were routed.

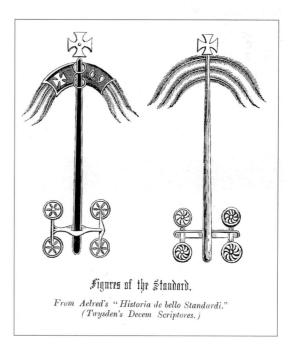

Figures of the Standard.

From Aelred's "Historia de bello Standardi."
(Twysden's Decem Scriptores.)

Before the Battle of the Standard, the fierce Scots had pillaged and desolated the land as they advanced south. The English leaders made the conflict into a Holy War and they constructed a religious standard which is represented here, in 1652, from a copy of a tall ship's mast mounted on a four-wheeled cart, with the mast surmounted by a silver pyx containing the Blessed Sacrament, on which the banners of St Peter of York, St John of Beverley and St Wilfred of Ripon were displayed.

Porch House, pictured in about 1900, is the oldest residential property in Northallerton, built by Richard Metcalfe in 1584. Charles I stayed here in completely different circumstances on two occasions: he was a guest of the Metcalfe family on 29 August 1640 and he dwelt here in February 1647 as a prisoner of the Parliamentary Commissioners. This was after part of his ransom had been paid by the English Parliament to the Scots – the receipt for £200,000 being signed on 21 January 1647 at Northallerton, and probably in Porch House.

Photographed in the 1960s the Fleece is certainly one of the oldest public houses in Northallerton, although it is hard to say exactly how ancient this quaint, stone-built popular edifice is. Charles Dickens visited here in the mid-nineteenth century and commented on the aged oaken ceiling beams. Originally on this site and taking up the two houses adjacent to the south, there was an Austin Friary, founded in 1340 with nine acres of land. Unfortunately nothing else is known of this religious house – except that the Austin Friars brewed beer!

This exquisite and detailed study of Northallerton market, seen to the north from outside the then Harewood Arms, was made in 1900 when Mrs Bonnett was proprietoress of the Golden Lion. The markets were a keystone of the town's economy from the very earliest times and according to a lease issued by the Bishop of Durham in 1772, his predecessors had been granted 'a Market every Wednesday' at Northallerton in 1127. Additionally, four important fairs were given: Candlemas, 14 February and St Bartholomew's, 6 September (both in 1200); St George's, 6 and 7 May (in 1554 – the forerunner of the present May Fair) and St Matthew's, 3 October (in 1609). Visitors such as William Camden (1586) and Daniel Defoe (1703) marvelled at the size of the fairs and even now the markets on Wednesdays and Saturdays are an essential element of Northallerton's commerce.

A fascinating sketch from 1841 delineates Northallerton railway coach station when the Darlington to York railway line opened on 30 March 1841. It was described by the *York Herald* as 'commodious and elegant built in the Elizabethan Gothic style'. As one of the original railway stations in the country, it is much regretted that not a vestige of it now remains. The arrival of the 'Iron Horse' ruined the stage coach industry, with the population of the town declining, dropping from 3,088 in 1841 to 2,870 in 1871, but with the consolidation of the railway hundreds of workers were employed, and in 1885 104 trains called on weekdays at Northallerton.

A photograph taken in 1890 features the Great North Road in the middle of its progress through Northallerton, a situation which had existed since time immemorial. This direct eastern route between London and Edinburgh carried the colourful stage-coach trade with famous coaches such as the 'Telegraph', 'Wellington' and 'Queen Charlotte' calling at the coaching inns, from 1770 to 1841 the main ones being the Golden Lion, King's Head, and Black Bull. Additionally, for centuries every military movement against Scotland by the English (and there were many) took this historic route.

When this print was produced in about 1860, Sun Beck flowed over the surface of Northallerton High Street and pedestrians crossed the road over the footbridge shown here, with a similar one across the road. Centrally featured is the notorious old Workhouse, in existence since 1720 for this purpose, before which it was the town's Guild Hall, built in 1444 by Cardinal Kemp. At the front of this building seven Northallerton men were hung for treason in 1570. In 1858 the inmates were relocated to the new Workhouse and the ancient Guild Hall building was demolished. The York Savings Bank was erected on the site in 1863; the building now houses Jefferson and Willan, Solicitors.

An old postcard of great interest, *c.* 1865, depicts the former Northallerton centre containing the butchers' Shambles, Market Cross and Toll Booth which were swept away in 1872 to make way for the Town Hall. The Toll Booth replaced the Guild Hall in 1720 as the centre of Northallerton affairs and from 1770 to 1785 the North Riding Quarter Sessions were held there. There were six shops on the ground floor and the town gaol (the 'Black Hole') was situated above with other rooms. Percy Hindmarsh bought the Market Cross for £5, but John Jefferson (Grace Gardner's maternal grandfather) obtained it, and returned it to the market-place in 1913.

Northallerton was given its initial impetus in becoming the North Riding county town when the North Riding Registry of Deeds was sited in Zetland Street – then very narrow with only a small entry to the High Street – in 1736. William Turner, the first Registrar (1736–53), had only one assistant – shades of the North Riding staff later! In 1782–83 the Registry was added to until it was as seen in this 1965 photograph, stretching down the north side of Zetland Street almost to the High Street. With the Registry completed, the North Riding magistrates erected a House of Correction, Governor's house and Court House nearby in 1785.

This 1910 postcard depicts the original, resplendent North Riding County Hall designed in a restrained Renaissance style by Walter Brierley of York at a cost of £33,264 16s 11d, with an extra £5,300 for the land which had been part of the football pitch on the Northallerton racecourse. It was officially opened on 31 January 1906 and wings were added to the north side in 1916 and to the south in 1930, and various additions have been made since then. The presence of the County Headquarters has been crucial to the development, economy and recent history of Northallerton.

PEOPLE & PLACES

Captain Thomas Hill of the North Yorkshire Rifles, seen here in about 1890, was appointed as the first Chief Constable of the North Riding of Yorkshire by the Quarter Sessions at Northallerton on 4 October 1856. It was a fortuitous selection because he directed and developed the embryonic police force with such dedication and acumen that it was an organization to be proud of when he retired at seventy-five on 31 September 1898. He lived at Romanby House where his son Alan was born, the latter gaining the Victoria Cross as a young Lieutenant at Majuba Hill, Transvaal on 27 February 1880. He remains the sole local winner of a VC.

The North Riding police force were most fortunate to attract Major Robert Bower as their Chief Constable when Thomas Hill retired. Major Bower had already been hailed in literature when his activities in Africa, as British Resident in Ibadan Tonga country, caused writer Edgar Wallace to model his legendary hero 'Sanders of the River' on him. He was *in situ* as Chief Constable from 1898 until his sudden death in 1929, during which time he revolutionized the force and obtained a new palatial Police Headquarters adjacent to the County Hall in 1909. He was knighted in 1925 amid universal acclaim.

A Wednesday market at Northallerton in the 1930s clearly shows that vans and small lorries had mainly replaced horses and carts. Of real interest are the buildings at the extreme right of the postcard: from right to left; Smithson's Stationers and Printers, the Three Tuns, Boston's the Grocer's and the Black Swan. All the businesses have now changed but at that time Boston's and Smithson's, run by two of the best-known Northallerton families, were among the foremost commercial operations in the town, and the Black Swan and Three Tuns were highly popular hostelries.

In 1911 Gladys Russell, Grace and Dudley Gardner pose on a tree trunk with the Gardner children's father, Ernest, below. He was the son of the legendary Captain George Gardner. Ernest was very successful in his own right as Northallerton's leading solicitor, North Riding coroner and the best-known amateur actor in the district. All the youngsters achieved in their own way: Gladys became an accomplished artist, having pictures 'hung' locally and nationally; Dudley was Northallerton's first aviator; and Grace was totally absorbed in welfare work, becoming the local WVS organizer and gaining lasting posterity by leaving a substantial amount of money – the Gardner Trust – for Northallerton's senior citizens.

This portrait of Wing Commander Dudley Gardner was reproduced from a drawing executed by Sir William Rothenstein in 1943 for the Air Ministry Portrait Gallery. Dudley, from Alverton, South Parade, Northallerton, was a legend in his own time, having been commissioned in the Green Howards (in 1914) and then seconded to the Royal Flying Corps, obtaining his pilot's wings in 1915. He then flew on the Western and other fronts, obtaining the King of Italy's Silver Medal for Valour and the Military Cross in January 1918 'for consistent and meritorious bravery'.

Dorothy Creighton Boston and Leslie Charles Barker pose outside Northallerton Parish Church after their wedding on 12 August 1937. The bridesmaids were Dorothy's sisters Gwen, Marie and Diana, the best man Ben Rider and the groomsmen Wilfred Barker and Herbert Sheldrake. Great interest was aroused locally because it brought together two of Northallerton's foremost commercial families. Their honeymoon was spent in Switzerland and their first home was the Old Hall, Thornton-le-Moor until moving to the well-known farm, Pasture House, south of Northallerton. Charles became managing director of Barkers of Northallerton which gained a reputation second to none.

A postcard of 1938 captures Northallerton's Wednesday market with heavy wooden canvas-topped stalls, large wicker baskets containing the vendors' goods and ice-cream at hand from DiPalma's tricycle. Centrally stands the sturdy and upright Market Cross dating from 1843. Traditionally the Market Cross is 'a signal for upright intention and fair dealing and designed as a check on worldly spirits'.

Carol Armstrong, seen in 1962, receiving the coveted Queen's Guide Award and citation. Behind her are two of the most prominent Guide leaders in Northallerton's history of the movement, left to right, Hilda Russell and Muriel Hird.

When Sir Hubert Thornley died in 1962 at his home, Register House, Northallerton, tributes flowed in both locally and nationally, and were summed up aptly by Sir Guy Ropner who said: 'It must be agreed that he was a very great man.' Hubert Thornley was appointed Clerk of the Peace and Clerk to the North Riding County Council aged thirty-two on 1 April 1916, and had unprecedented influence over North Riding for the next forty-two years. He uniquely attended 165 consecutive Quarter Sessions, was awarded the CBE in 1949 and the final accolade of a knighthood in 1958 was 'applauded far beyond the county border'.

Romanby Road, viewed in about 1948, was originally part of the Great North Road as it came from the Old Turnpike Road (Malpas Road) to veer left as it met the High Street. In the old coaching days, three public houses were on this short route: the Leopard (protruding out on the left at the end of Arncliffe Terrace), the New Inn and the Durham Ox facing each other on the Romanby Road and High Street corners.

Thirsk Road, pictured in the late 1930s, was the other main road from the south and in the stagecoach days it was turnpiked from York to Northallerton at Burton Stone, Skelton, Stockhill Green, Thirsk and Purgatory – the bars being set up by 1780. It entered Northallerton on the Thirsk Road, as viewed here, but without the houses which were built from 1900 onwards. The house where the author and his four brothers and three sisters were brought up is shrouded by trees, but is immediately to the right of the telegraph pole in the foreground.

The Northallerton Weighell family in 1917 during the First World War. Standing, left to right: Lily, Thomas (a Staff Sergeant in the Royal Engineers and later father of Maurice, Sidney, Elma and Brenda), Elsie, Robert, Hammond (a Corporal) and Annie. Seated: Mrs Fanny Weighell (mother), Nora and Mr William Weighell (father). The family were strongly featured in Sidney Weighell's book *A Hundred Years of Railway Weighells*.

The motor car is coming more to the fore in Northallerton market-place in about 1925, although the horse still has a place, as witnessed in the distance on the main road. Seated at the Market Cross the men are putting the town to rights and the Town Hall and Lewis and Cooper's are particularly well defined. Of great interest is the building on the extreme right occupied on the ground floor by two shops, Pearson's the butchers being that on the right. Until about 1855 when it closed through lack of custom, this was the King's Head hotel which in the old coaching days rivalled the Golden Lion as the major inn.

At the Northallerton Gala in 1958, which was attended by over 3,000 people, Vina Galloway was a very popular choice as Miss Northallerton. Two of the judges on this memorable occasion were Paul Massie, the Canadian film star and Anthony Asquith, the famous film director who made the locally based *Way to the Stars* in 1944. Vina had been Head Girl at the Allertonshire School and then embarked on a most successful artistic career as a teacher of dance, getting numerous protégés through examinations and founding an excellent Dance Ensemble which undertook regular engagements.

NORTHALLERTON AT WAR

*When the Second World War broke out in September
1939, the British public were exhorted by their
Government to 'Dig for Victory' and produce their own
food. This is one of the advertising leaflets circulated
around Northallerton and the local citizens responded
wholeheartedly, turning their immaculate lawns and
blooming flowerbeds into vegetable patches.*

Lending a hand to the war effort in late 1940 are the Northallerton Girl Guides, collecting surplus aluminium and handing it to Mr C.B. Eyre to stack on to his lorry. The scene is outside the ivy-clad Northallerton Urban District Offices, now the Northallerton Divisional Police Headquarters. The major part of the Government directive to gather scrap metal concerned railings and shortly after this the vast majority of Northallerton's railings were dismantled, much to the consternation of most townsfolk.

The Red Cross and St John's Ambulancemen mainly form this group who comprised a major part of the Northallerton Air Raid Precautions (ARP) team. Behind the party is an ARP ambulance. The ARP Headquarters was in Boston's yard and, interestingly, the boy at the front left wears the uniform of St Bede's College, Sunderland – a reminder that in 1940 the evacuees from Sunderland and Gateshead were an important factor in the town. Standing, left to right: Charlie Burley, Mr Dawson, Dr Davey (in civvies), Fred Thompson, Mr Asquith, Mr Carr. Kneeling in uniform: Arthur Collins, Wilf King.

The North Riding 5th Battalion, D Company, Army Cadet Force (Northallerton), Green Howards, winners of the Small Bore Shooting Competition for the Jackson Rose Bowl, 1942. Back row, left to right: Derek Bell, George Darwin, Bill Eden (instructor), George Paley, Alan Eden. Front row: Maurice Archer, David Robinson.

Army Cadet Force, 5th Battalion, D Company, Green Howards, Northallerton at the Allertonshire School were formed in May 1942. The photograph includes: Captain George Gardner, Staff Sergeant Bill Eden, Warrant Officer Jones, Basil Young, Alan Eden, Geoff Blair, Alan Bell, Tom Ward, Arthur Snowdon, Derek Bell, George Darwin, Maurice Archer, George Paley, Bill Bratley, Bill Boston.

Kellett and Pick Ministry of Defence workshop, 1943–4, employed local men who serviced military vehicles. Back row, left to right: -?-, -?-, G. Barker, H. Wetherall, F. Eyles, H. Hunton, Mr Reason, -?-, B. Joblin. Middle row: -?-, D. Archer, -?-, G. Brannigan, K. Book, D. Bell, K. Askwith, K. Ward, D. Baldwin, Mr Warder. Third row: F. Wright, H. Smith, L. Gent, G. Sunley, G. Forth, J. Clark. Front row, left to right: D. Pollit, E. Smart, G. Wilson, Mr Heap (manager), W. Watson, E. Warder.

Tony Lyons of Brompton was on the battleship HMS *Duke of York* in 1943 when this photograph was taken. He was 'present and correct' at the ship's company inspection.

George Law of Hatfield Road, Northallerton joined the Royal Air Force Volunteer Reserve in 1940 and is seen in his flying suit outside an aerodrome billet. Soon after this he was killed, flying as a Navigator, and in this volume, represents the twenty brave ex-Northallerton Grammar School pupils who made the supreme sacrifice on active service during the Second World War. George was intelligent, caring, patriotic and popular and, like the others, was a great loss to the community.

A Handley Page Halifax, photographed on the runway at RAF Leeming in 1944, when the Royal Canadian Air Force Squadrons, Lion (No. 427) and Bison (No. 429), were stationed there, equipped with Halifaxes from 1943 until 1945. The Canadian personnel developed a tremendous rapport with the Northallerton and other local people, life-long friendships were made and Yorkshire girls married young Canadians. The attrition rate and sacrifice in the Halifaxes were almost incomprehensible as RAF Leeming lost 161 Halifaxes and 903 aircrew in two years.

CANADIAN PACIFIC TELEGRAPHS
World Wide Communications

STANDARD TIME INDICATED

C.D.1

W.D.NEIL, GENERAL MANAGER OF COMMUNICATIONS. MONTREAL

```
2WA.   RO.   40/39 GB 2 EX REPORT DELIVERY-

OTTAWA ONT DEC 5TH 324AM 1943

MR W.M.BEATTY,
                        967
417 CAMPBELL ST.,

WINNIPEG MAN.

M9461 DEEPLY REGRET TO ADVISE THAT YOUR SON R ONE FIVE TWO EIGHT SEVEN NINE

FLIGHT SERGEANT JAMES MURRAY BEATTY WAS KILLED ON ACTIVE SERVICE OVERSEAS

DECEMBER SECOND STOP PLEASE ACCEPT MY PROFOUND SYMPATHY STOP LETTER FOLLOWS.

                        RCAF CASUALTIES OFFICER.
```

At 1430 hours, on 2 December 1943, Halifax V DJ932 K-King took off from RCAF 1664 Conversion Unit Croft on a routine training flight. Half an hour later K-King was a crumpled mass of burning debris in Springwell Lane, Northallerton with all the crew of four Canadians, two Ulstermen and a Welshman dead in the wreckage. The sensation was magnified because the stricken aircraft was within yards of crashing on the Applegarth Council School where all the children, aged five to nine, of the town were engaged in afternoon lessons. But for a minimal distance, the tragedy would have been indescribable and everyone in Northallerton that day has indelible memories. A technical fault caused the crash. The accident telegram concerns Flight Sergeant James Beatty and informs his next of kin in Winnipeg. He was Navigator of the doomed plane, aged only twenty, and is buried with his three Canadian colleagues at Harrogate.

Her Royal Highness the Duchess of Gloucester, as the Commandant of the Women's Auxiliary Air Force, visited Royal Canadian Air Force Leeming on 14 October 1943. After inspecting the WAAF personnel, accompanied by Squadron Officer Joyce Litman, she lunched in the Officers' Mess and is here signing the visitors' book overlooked by the Commanding Officer, Group Captain J.L. Plant.

This is the pleasant calm before the storm for Sergeant Tommy Riordan of the Royal Engineers (the author's eldest brother) aged nineteen, seen holding two photogenic French poodles outside his quarters at Harnes near Lille, France in November 1939. He was with the British Expeditionary Force which was soon involved in the great escape from Dunkirk in May 1940. He was wounded in the eye and hand in the retreat to the coast. Eventually he was repatriated by boats from Le Pas and taken to a Manchester hospital. But the men of the BEF lived to fight another day and Tom was awarded the Military Medal at the Battle of Monte Cassino, Italy in 1944.

Northallerton's Harry Thompson stands on the extreme right in this most unusual photograph. He is in a Burmese workshop where he was in charge of the Japanese prisoners of war, posing with him in 1946.

Another rare photograph from about 1944 shows three German prisoners of war who worked at Pearson's South Thornborough Farm, Thirsk Road during the Second World War. Left to right they are 'Ernest', Günter Klein Schmidt and 'August'. Günter was particularly popular on the farm and corresponded long after the war with the Pearsons. The German POWs were accommodated in a camp at Stone Cross.

This VE party was held in May 1945 at Rose Cottage (adjacent to Malpas Road) for all nearby children. Their mothers stand happily behind them. The children identified are: front row, left to right: Marjorie Martin, Avis McCuin, Joyce Render, -?-, -?-, -?-, -?-, Margaret Wright, -?-, -?-, -?-, -?-, June Berry, Dorothy Watson. Second row: Wilma Fawcett, Jean Carter, -?-, -?-, -?-, Kathleen Stockdale, Anne Carter, Ann Pashby, David Wright, Alan McCuin, Richard Pashby, Keith Wilbor.

There were several more VE parties in Northallerton in May 1945 and this one features all the parents and children of Quaker Lane. They are celebrating in the premises behind Quaker Lane, which then belonged to Willoughby the builders and Sam Turner's (the 'Farmers Friend') and which are now occupied by Swain Court.

Susan Carol Riordan

DIEU ET MON DROIT

8th June, 1946

To-DAY, AS WE CELEBRATE VICTORY, I send this personal message to you and all other boys and girls at school. For you have shared in the hardships and dangers of a total war and you have shared no less in the triumph of the Allied Nations.

I know you will always feel proud to belong to a country which was capable of such supreme effort; proud, too, of parents and elder brothers and sisters who by their courage, endurance and enterprise brought victory. May these qualities be yours as you grow up and join in the common effort to establish among the nations of the world unity and peace.

George R.I.

All the primary school children received these citations from King George VI regarding the war in 1946. This particular one was received by Susan Riordan (the author's youngest sister) along with the other Applegarth and East Road pupils – the only primary schools then.

THE HOSPITAL TRADITION

Hospitals and hospitality are deeply rooted in Northallerton's history — St James' Hospital was founded eight hundred years ago, one mile from the then centre of town, on the Thirsk Road. Now Spital Farm occupies the site and clear remains of the medieval hospital can be seen in this photograph in the fabric of the farmhouse and wall. In 1244 St James' had a Master and twenty other staff caring for thirteen patients (mainly with leprosy) and feeding thirty local poor people nightly. By the time the hospital was dissolved in 1540, it had considerable landholdings around Northallerton from benefactors and these lands were diverted by Henry VIII to endow Christ Church College, Oxford.

During the First World War the North Riding County Hall became a Red Cross hospital of thirty-two beds (ten reserved for Green Howards) and by the end of the war 750 patients had been nursed back to health. This postcard is most valuable because it was written by a patient to his daughter Kathleen in Doncaster on 11 November 1918 – Armistice Day. Northallerton County Hall was marked with a cross to indicate his ward, and he comments on the comfortable beds, also praising the Red Cross nurses.

The Northallerton Friarage Hospital derives its name from the Carmelite Friary which was on the hospital site from 1356 to 1539. Here the gate of the Friary is seen incised into the wall of the lemonade factory at the southern end of Brompton Road, latterly belonging to Swains until it was closed in 1956. Unfortunately, soon after this, the factory and wall were swept away and the only visible remains now of the Friary is the stone wall at the south-east of Brompton Road and nearby stone slabs, many with ornamental etchings.

Pictured here in about 1880 is the oldest edifice of the Friarage Hospital complex – the Northallerton Union Workhouse. It was opened in 1858 and has given its architectural lines to the resplendent new phases of the hospital, built in the 1980s and 1990s. Of interest are the wall of the adjacent Northallerton Show Field (1867 to 1933) and Sun Beck, running openly down Bullamoor Road.

An accident of war created the Friarage Hospital when an Emergency Hospital was built in 1939–40 on Friarage Fields by Government directive, in case the civilian population of Teesside was bombed. To expediate matters, eight wooden wards for 277 beds were brought from Canada in units of Oregon pine with cedarwood cladding, and were assembled on concrete plinths. One of the hutted wards is seen here. These wards have become almost legendary because fifty-six years later these 'temporary measures' are still fulfilling an important role in the hospital.

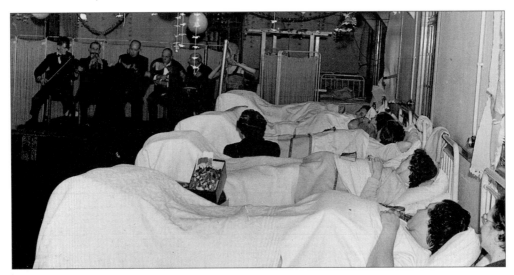

The inside of a wooden ward at Christmas time in the early 1950s when ladies in the Woman's Ward at the Friarage Hospital were being serenaded by a musical ensemble organized by Toc H, who did many good works for the hospital's patients. Other regular Christmas hospital happenings were the procession through the wards by the Northallerton Parish Church choir led by the inimitable Gerry Wilson and the annual gift distribution by Father Christmas, a role filled most adequately by Albert Gaskell for over twenty years.

At the nurses' graduation ceremony of 1959 nineteen nurses graduated, including Patricia Norman, who won the Inman Gold medal, the sole male J.R. 'Bobby' Cooper, Brenda Watson, Judy Simpson, Jean Palmer, Audrey Stevenson, Mary Easby, Audrey Lilley, Margaret Potter, Molly Barker, Pam Colvin, Maureen Smart, and Kathleen Hutchinson. On the stage are, back row, left to right: Mr Appleton (second), Mr Blair Edmunds (third) and Dr McKenzie, (fifth) and on the front row: Mrs Rawlings, Miss Gibson, Mr Gilbert Parker, -?-, John Westwood Adamson (chairman), Cassie Harker (matron) and Mrs Constantine. To put the record straight, Gilbert Parker was the senior consultant who founded the civilian hospital in 1948.

In the Second World War from 1 January 1943 to November 1947 the Friarage became Royal Air Force Hospital Northallerton and this integral connection with flying was presaged on the site in July 1913 by Gustav Hamel, seen in this postcard starting his aeroplane by swinging its propellor. He flew several enthusiasts on 'flips' over the town in his 50 hp Bleriot monoplane at the Northallerton Carnival held on the then Show Field, at Friarage Fields. Unfortunately Hamel's life was cut short because the next year he simply disappeared while flying over the English Channel.

In these days of advanced medical science and equipment, this apparatus seems antediluvian but when this X-ray machinery was presented to the Rutson Hospital by Mrs Constantine of Harlsey Hall in 1932, it was greeted with great enthusiasm as bringing the local hospital up to date.

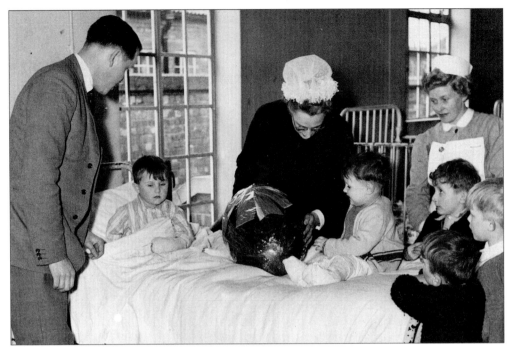

At Easter in 1955 in the children's ward at the Friarage Hospital, the Matron, Cassie Harker, shows a giant Easter egg to eager children gathering round; Sister Dorothy Sawyer looks on. The scene illustrates the friendly and caring spirit which has always characterized the Friarage, most especially where children are concerned.

Lady Hunter of Howden Gate, Northallerton, the wife of Sir Ellis Hunter, presented the Awards at the customary annual Nurses' Graduation Ceremony in September 1953. She is seen congratulating Nurse Doris Hudson on her receipt of the Inman Gold Medal as the most successful student. John Weston Adamson, chairman of the Hospital Management Committee, looks on in the centre with Matron Cassie Harker on the left and the Bishop of Whitby, the Right Revd W.H. Baddeley on the right.

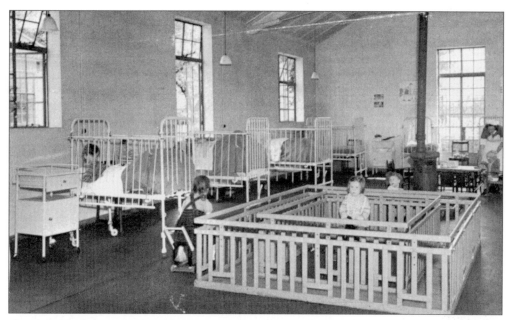

This is the Friarage Hospital children's ward again, this time for the younger children. Ever since the foundation of the peacetime civilian hospital in 1948 and the influx of its first patients – young polio sufferers – the Friarage had gained a reputation for its care of children, which has continued throughout its subsequent history. A feature of this photograph, taken in about 1955, is the large black coke-stove in the background. Every ward had three such stoves which were replenished and riddled three times a day until a central boiler replaced the antiquated coke system in the early 1960s.

Posing during a brief break at the Friarage Hospital in 1955 are five popular and well-known staff nurses. Left to right: Miss Wheatley, Ruth Taylor, Molly Boyes, Jane Groves and Dorothy Sawyer.

Formed in 1958 the Friarage Hospital League of Friends has been a great asset to the hospital, raising funds through almost every organization and community in the widespread hospital catchment area. The Friarage fête, held annually in the summertime, has raised thousands of pounds and dates back to the early 1950s. Captured here is one of the earliest fêtes, held outside the Sunbeck House building. Some patients have been wheeled down in their beds to savour the atmosphere.

TRANSPORT

*John Ernest Hutton, the only son of John Hutton of
Solberge Hall, was a great entrepreneur despite his young
age. In 1899 he introduced electric lighting to
Northallerton, driving round to supervise the
installations in the first car ever to be used regularly in
Northallerton. He then began to build cars at his
workshops, Ohm Electric Works, situated at the North
End of the town near to the Wesleyan Church. He was
helped for a time by C.S. Rolls before the latter went to
Derby to collaborate with Royce to form the world-famous
Rolls-Royce firm. Hutton built two cars, the Voiturette
and Simplex in 1900 – the latter being shown here.*

Jervaulx was one of the several idiosyncratic small stations on the Northallerton to Garsdale Wensleydale railway line. This study from about 1890 is arresting for its quaintness and characters as well as for the fact that there must have been few monasteries nationally with their own railway station!

Leeming Bar railway staff – an astonishing ten in all, c. 1910. Qualifying the staffing complement, the station also controlled the level crossing over the main north–south road (Leeming Lane and, after 1924, the A1 road), adjacent to the railway station. This was always a difficult crossing to man but it became increasingly so with the gradual and then tremendous build up of motor vehicles.

This descriptive photograph, taken in February 1954, encapsulates Northallerton's position as a busy main-line station on the great eastern London to Edinburgh route and as a railway junction with local traffic. A main-line steam train is surging into Northallerton station, passing the now demolished signal box. When it was first opened in September 1939, however, it was the most modern in the country. A shunting engine is bustling about and the branch lines are visible to Teesside on the right and Wensleydale on the left.

Northallerton railway station, seen in 1956, was a solid substantial structure and a very busy place. There were many railway rooms and also a well-patronized W.H. Smith's booksellers and newsagents and a restaurant of high-quality used greatly by the townsfolk, particularly the nearby County Hall staff. The glass roof-canopy can be seen in the background down the south-bound platform with a similar one running down the northern side. Seemingly indestructible, it was all demolished in 1985 and replaced with small waiting rooms on each main platform.

This delightful postcard from the 1920s gently pokes fun at the Northallerton–Wensleydale line, the engine – 'Old Faithful' as it was affectionately known – its crew and followers. In Northallerton the engine was playfully called the 'Bedale Pusher' but like the postcard, the mood was of appreciation for the line which was a legend in its own lifetime.

There was great consternation when the Government decided to close the Northallerton–Garsdale line to passenger traffic but despite protests the last journey up the Dales was the 4.10 p.m. from Northallerton on Saturday 24 August 1954. Several passengers travelled for sentimental reasons and the engine and crew are captured here on this historic journey. From right to left: Ron May, Low Gates, Northallerton, driver; Derek Appleby, Thirsk, fireman and the guard, George Ezzard. The small boy on the right is not named.

Engine locomotive sheds existed at Northallerton for well over a century, situated in the low-level line area immediately below the main line north-bound platform. Not long after this photograph was taken by Ron Bateson in 1952 the sheds were closed, the workers made redundant and eventually the locomotive sheds were demolished. In the railway's heyday over 500 railway workers were employed in the town with many living at Romanby.

Another invaluable industrial photograph of 1952 shows the engine sheds but of particular interest is the old low-level temporary platform built during the war to facilitate troop movements. Again, it has long since gone.

Willow Beck overflowed in 1931, flooding the North End at Northallerton. Here a typical motorbus of the time is making a valiant effort to carry its passengers northwards. Also in shot is the North End goods station which was a thriving business then. In 1850 it was originally a passenger station on the Leeds to Hartlepool line rivalling the original Northallerton station, but the respective companies merged and the North End station became used purely for goods. Incidentally the goods station was cannon-shelled by the Luftwaffe in March 1945.

Accident scenes involving motor vehicles became more and more familiar as the twentieth century progressed and here on 4 July 1960 the police are assessing the crash between a large Rover car and a motor cycle and sidecar (hidden behind the car) at the Thirsk Road–South Parade junction. The first motor accident in Northallerton was in 1899 when Ernest Hutton's car frightened a horse. Of note is the configuration of houses on the left before the East Road–High Street link road.

OCCUPATIONS

Standing next to the boiler he maintained at Baxter's Brewery, Thornton-le-Moor, is James Foster, the great-grandfather of Dr David Severs of Northallerton (who supplied the photograph) and his brothers John, Keith and Peter, c. 1880.

In 1901 the Railway Hotel near Northallerton station was rebuilt by Dan Oakley and his men. Dan, having come from Durham to fulfil the contract, remained at Northallerton throughout his working life. Second from the right, he is posing here with his plastering team in front of the hotel which was later renamed the Station Hotel. Before the railway in 1841 it was called the Horse and Jockey, as it was adjacent to Northallerton Racecourse.

When Dan Oakley Ltd built the United Auto Services Bus Station in 1937 on the south-eastern corner of Brompton Road they discovered a considerable amount of excavated material. This undoubtedly consisted of the remains of the Carmelite Friary previously on the site. To clear away the debris, as indicated by the photograph, they used both old and new methods – a donkey and buggy, horses and carts and a lorry! Dan Oakley's firm constructed many important buildings between the two World Wars.

Agriculture, naturally, has been the prime industry in the Northallerton area from time immemorial and some engaging studies are offered as representative of this. Here, typical of the 1920s, Lawrence Newcombe is ploughing with two handsome horses at Deighton.

Charlie Galley farmed on the north side of Northallerton before the Second World War and is seen holding his prize bull. He was the uncle of Ernest Pearson of South Thornborough who supplied this and other arresting photographs.

Robert Newcombe stands at Deighton crossroads in 1920, sturdily ready for agricultural action, and fully equipped for haymaking with a scythe and hay fork. He dramatically symbolizes the old methods and breed of men, contrasting completely with the mechanization of modern farming today.

Undoubtedly the likes of this will never be seen again – a three-horse-led reaping team at Longlands Farm, south of Northallerton, with each individual having specific roles to fill. Longlands previously belonged to Christ Church College, Oxford and before this, St James' Hospital. The personnel in 1920 are, left to right: Rowland Harrison, Tom Hammond, Mrs Hammond and John Hart, driving the team.

In July 1918 Louis Newcombe, aged eleven, sits proudly on his mount while Lawrence Newcombe, aged fifteen, holds the pony's head at Deighton. In those days, before the general use of the internal combustion engine, horses and ponies were the essential mode of transport for the various members of the farm.

The North Riding and South Durham Executive of the National Farmers' Union was the most powerful farming body in the area and its members, with some of their friends, pose for the camera in June 1939. Top row, left to right: H. Barnett, J.E. Kirkup, W.G. Johnson, W. Sanderson, R.M. Hodgson, L. Winn, J. Foster. Second row: M. Keenlyside, H.H. Holmes, R. Allen, R.H. Chappell, J.W. Raine, F. Foster, E.A. Almack, J. Percival, L.C. Webster, C.M. Fawcett, J.P. Foster, J.R. Dale, -?-, W.T. Raw, -?-, W. Almack, E.W. Barley, J.H. Wrightson. Third row: C. Nesom, H. Oxley, W.S. Cook, D.H. Chapman, J.T. Allison, G. Kendrew, T.W. Spilman, J.G. Harris, W. Lowther, R. Johnson, F.C. Johnson, D.S. Hendrie. Front row: H. Potts, W. Sanderson, A.A. Medd, C.R. Hawthorn, J.D. Young, M. Readman, G.F. Ward, A.C. Trenchman, J. McNeil, J.T. Raper, J. Brodie, W. Farndale, W.L. Prest, J.R. Harrison.

Another farming art being practised at Great Smeaton in 1910, when sheep shearing was in full spate.

At the hub of the agricultural and indeed the area's economy was the age-old Northallerton market. Here is a typical Wednesday market scene in the 1920s. It is interesting to note the cluster of 'hooded' cars, the horse and trailer mingling with the motor cars, the bicycle in the middle of the road and the exceptionally poor quality of the High Street road surface.

This emigration notice appeared in *Smithson's Northallerton Almanack* of 1912 and similar advertisements were frequent from 1890 to 1914. Life on the land was precarious and many emigrated from the Northallerton area — mainly to Canada and the United States — in search of a better life for themselves and their families, an object in which many were successful.

Buying and selling livestock has always been crucial to farmers and in this colourful scene at the Applegarth Mart in 1948 M.W. Darwin and Sons, one of the leading local auctioneering firms, conducted the sale for Northallerton Auctions. Maurice Darwin started his concern in the 1930s and he was joined by his sons John and George after the Second World War. Here Maurice Darwin (auctioneer) is standing at the back, on his right is George Darwin (clerk) and the hatted John Darwin is on George's right. Some well-known farmers present are M. Pattison, L. Barker, F. Chester and J. Lister.

Darwin's Poultry Sales have become synonymous with Christmastide at Northallerton, when the Town Hall is festooned with birds and buyers come from far and wide. This is one of the earlier sales; there have now been over forty consecutive occasions. At the Town Hall in 1955 are, left to right: Mrs B. Langthorne (Brompton), George Darwin (auctioneer), H. Smith (Leeming), Mrs P. Greenwood (Bedale), John Warrior (Bedale) and John Darwin.

Soon after the Second World War, Darwins started to hold sales for the Ministry of Agriculture, selling tractors and agricultural machinery in fields off Lees Lane and then Ainderby Road. Maurice Darwin is standing on a tractor in 1948 to conduct such a sale aided by son John, in the foreground doing the clerical work, with over 1,000 farmers in attendance.

Darwin's also specialized in furniture sales and on 23 April 1965 they auctioned 450 lots of furniture at Thorp Perrow Hall, Bedale, on the instructions of Sir Guy Ropner MC. This hall had once been the home of Richmondshire's first MP in 1885, Sir Frederick Milbank, and currently it is becoming increasingly famous for its superb arboretum. Estate agency was Darwin's other field of expertise – a profession which expanded rapidly with the housing boom when several new firms came to Northallerton.

> **THORP PERROW HALL**
> **BEDALE**
>
> By order of Sir Leonard Ropner, BT., M.C.
>
> ## CATALOGUE
>
> *of*
>
> *The Valuable contents removed from a London Residence and Furniture, surplus to requirements*
>
> *of*
>
> # THORP PERROW HALL
>
> ## BEDALE, YORKS.
>
> *To be sold by Auction in a marquee on the Premises*
>
> *on*
>
> ### Friday, 23rd April, 1965
>
> **COMMENCING PROMPTLY AT 10-30 a.m.**
>
> *by*
>
> **M. W. DARWIN & SONS**
>
> 140 HIGH STREET - NORTHALLERTON.
>
> Telephone 3567.
>
> Refreshments   Catalogue Price 1/6

The Urban District Council refuse lorry is collecting rubbish down South Parade in 1932, as part of its quota of emptying 800 ash bins and 112 closet pails as well as 49 dry ashpits and 23 privy ashpits per month. This indicates the inadequate sanitation in the yards but this situation was infinitely better than in 1900 when Dr Baigent exclaimed: 'The yards are appalling, disgusting, unsanitary and indecent'. Approximately thirty men were employed by Northallerton UDC.

Banks have played a vital role in Northallerton's commercial activities since the nineteenth century especially when the York County Savings Bank was built on the renowned site of the Guild Hall and the workhouse. It was opened on 17 May 1862. Almost a century later, the bank staff are gathered on 24 March 1955 to mark the completion of the first million-pound deposits. Left to right are Doreen Forth (Newcombe), Rupert Halderthay (local actuary), Shirley Wilkinson (Taylor), Charles Lawton (chief actuary), Barbara Rose (Tiffin).

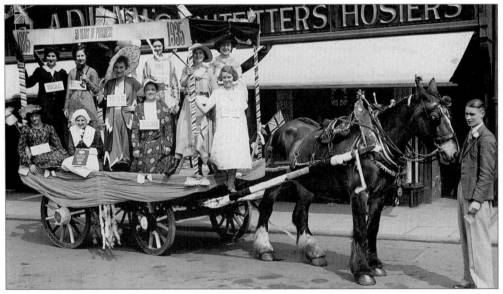

This attractive carnival float was made in 1935 in celebration of Clapham's the draper's jubilee, (1885–1935). It is standing outside Clapham's shop with several happy employers aboard. Holding the horse's head is Stanley Forth of Brompton who married Gladys Simmons, at the rear of the float. There is a sad end to the story, however, because Stanley Forth, serving as a sergeant in the Coldstream Guards during the Second World War, laid down his life at Anzio, Italy in February 1944, much to the grief of his close family and the many friends of this likeable young man.

John W. Clapham's shop is pictured in 1925, just after the shop front had been remodelled. The staff are standing in the doorways and Clapham's Yard is at the extreme right. This was a tremendous achievement because he started off as an apprentice to George Oxendale, went to the USA for experience where he slept with a gun under his pillow in Jacksonville before returning home to build his business from scratch. He obtained a shop with one bow-window and extended his premises in 1890 and 1902 to its eventual size.

By total contrast Clapham's is seen here with its modern façade in 1960 being kept up with the new trends and standards by John's son Jack, managing director, aided by Norman and John Clapham (grandsons) who were directors. A notable addition was the provision of a café added by expanding the building out to the rear. In 1963 Clapham's was merged with Upton's, the old-established Middlesbrough firm and in 1977, the shop was conveyed to Boyes' whose multi-faceted store still flourishes on the site.

A very quaint photograph taken in 1910 of the Wensleydale Pure Milk Society at Northallerton. It is seen here in its embryonic state (it was formed in 1905), consisting of a single building with a gantry adjacent to the Wensleydale–Northallerton railway line to facilitate milk distribution. The cows in the field are prophetic as later Cow and Gate bought the firm!

By 1956 the milk factory and its buildings, personnel, functions and objectives had been totally revolutionized. It had diversified into making milk products such as cheese, cream and powdered milk and milk distribution by rail was gradually being replaced by lorries and tankers. After its earliest beginnings it became part of Dried Milk Products, and then in 1932 it was taken over by the prestigious Cow and Gate organization which merged with United Dairies Limited in the 1960s to form Unigate.

Eileen Thompson, left, and Dorothy Lyons, right, stand outside the Black Swan public house in the 1930s. It was closed on 31 December 1986 with Mrs Featherstone as the last landlady. The licensed trade had always been an essential part of the town's economy and social expression, it having a national reputation for its ale. However, between 1850 and 1986, no fewer than eighteen Northallerton pubs had closed, with only one replacement, the Jolly Minister in 1958.

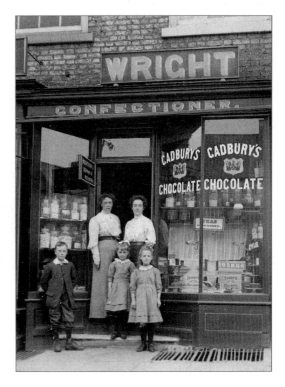

An attractive photograph of Wright's Confectioners, 1910. The shop is situated on the east side of the High Street near the Town Hall, since owned by Ankers and recently occupied by 'Affections'. At the rear, left to right: Miss Sarah Jane Wright and Miss Emma Mary Wright, both of whom lived down Lascelles Lane. At the front are their nephew and nieces: Victor Wright (Pearl Lynas' father) and his sisters Ivy and Violet Wright.

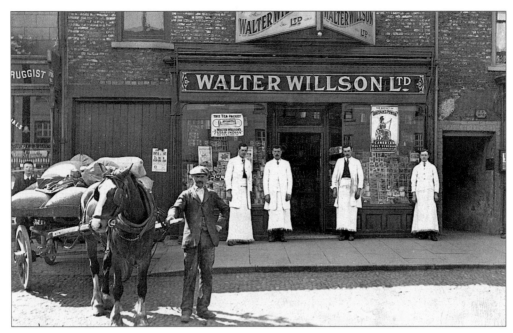

Another shop to emphasize the strong retailing character of Northallerton is Walter Willson's grocery shop seen here in 1913. Mr Boyes, Mr Glover (manager) Mr Harrison and Mr Gamble stand, left to right, in front of the shop and Mr Sunley holds the shop's horse, Tommy. Noticeable is the large commercial ·entrance door on the left and a typical yard entry is seen clearly on the right. Walter Willson's site was eventually taken over by 'Betty's' (café and shop) in the 1970s which has won national accolades for its high standards.

This group posing at the entrance to the North Riding County Hall in about 1950 is the North Riding County Treasurer's Department, including many well-known Northallerton personalities. Jim Holmes is on the front extreme left with Lloyd Dales next to him; the County Treasurer, Mr Wormald is sixth left on the front and immediately behind him in a dark suit is Matthew Cook. In consideration of this large department, which was only one of many, it is a timely reminder that in Northallerton and its environs the County Council was, and is, the largest single employer.

YARDS, STREETS & BUILDINGS

Market Row in 1956, facing towards the exit to the High Street, one of the foremost, best-built and well-kept yards in the town. It was also a main thoroughfare between the High Street and the Applegarth, inclusive of the Applegarth School. Although still named Market Row it now houses the incomparable Barker's Arcade with its attractive decor and high quality shops. This modern arcade was created by demolishing both the old Market Row and Hudson's yard adjacent to the south.

The west side of East Road in 1950 featuring a conglomeration of buildings and at least two inhabited houses with a large Guinness advertising sign as the centrepiece! When the slum clearance programme of the late 1950s and 1960s commenced, all these buildings were taken down and a rectangular modern edifice of offices and flats – which itself has suffered criticism because of its angular lines and apparent lack of subtlety – was erected.

An intriguing collage of posters advertising numerous events, led by 'Goldilocks and the Three Bears', occupies the wall of this one-storey building at the end of the south side of Zetland Street in 1962. Posters (which seem to have replaced the 'bell man'!) were a regular feature of pre-1965 Northallerton as the main advertising process. One of the leading poster placers was Harry Render who did the job virtually as a hobby, carrying on an ancient family tradition.

The inevitable knot of spectators gather to witness the start of the demolition of the yards, *c*. 1958. This one is believed to be Clapham's Yard. Unquestionably this obliteration of buildings and slums was the greatest social revolution of the last two centuries.

In 1968, when the demolition of yards and buildings on the east side of the town was in progress, these brick vaults were uncovered in the area where Club Amadeus now stands. They were believed to be about 200 years old and a theory was advanced that they were the brick kilns of the North Riding House of Correction (gaol) in 1785. However, it seems more likely that they were the wine vaults for a hotel or public house on the High Street.

On the west side of the High Street, in the process of being demolished in about 1965, this yard uncovers
a typical 'one up, one down house of the kind which hundreds of families in Northallerton lived in for at
least the last two centuries. The downstairs held the fire, oven and the staircase, and all the family slept
upstairs – irrespective of numbers.

Meadow Lane off Bullamoor Road, photographed in 1965, was typical of where the people who had lost
their yard homes were re-housed; a series of neat houses with their own gardens. By 1971 the Town
Clerk, Percy Hartley – the mainspring behind the building revolution – stated that no fewer than 1,500
council houses had been built by Northallerton Urban District Council since 1949, chiefly in the
Bullamoor area.

This is one of the last photographs of the North Riding Register Office's tree-lined High Street entrance, with its wrought-iron gates and flanking houses, before they were bulldozed to the ground in September 1968. Even the protestations by the Northallerton Urban District Council that the gates were rotten failed to appease the disappointment of the public.

This public perturbation continued with the demolition of Miss Lee's confectionery and cake shop and much of the Register Office, both seen here on Zetland Street in early 1968. For a time the site remained vacant until the Yorkshire Bank and an adjoining shop were built. Of all the redevelopment programmes this was by far the most controversial.

Southlands, the former residence of Alan and Mrs Rider, at the southern extremity of the High Street, was in a derelict state here in the 1960s. It had seen fine former days under the Riders – Alan being managing director of the Vale of Mowbray bacon factory at Leeming Bar, a county councillor and First World War Military Medal holder. Soon after Southlands was demolished several houses to its immediate north were also knocked down to make way for the High Street–East Road link road and the North Yorkshire County Library Headquarters which opened in 1977.

A postcard from about 1925 shows an almost traffic-free High Street and an attractive ive-clad building immediately to the south of the Durham Ox. This house belonged to Mrs Caffin and family who relocated here from the Vicarage in 1896 when her husband, Revd Bernard C. Caffin, the Vicar of Northallerton, died. In 1931 the Caffins' house was demolished so that the present post office could be built on the site by Dan Oakley Limited, and the Caffin family moved to Bedale.

Northallerton became the established County Town of the North Riding of Yorkshire when, after the siting of the Registry in 1736, further North Riding County buildings, the House of Correction and the Court House were erected to the instructions of John Carr of York in 1785 at Priest's Garth, which contained a horse pond. The original Court House was rebuilt in 1880 and by the time this photograph was taken in the 1950s over 500 Quarter Sessions had been held on the site.

Also much needed had been a modern Registry of Deeds, and this was built facing the County Hall on Racecourse Lane by Dan Oakley at a cost of £12,546 in 1927. This picture was taken in 1946. A new Court House was constructed adjacent and to the east of the Registry in 1937.

When the North Riding police constabulary was formed in 1856 under Thomas Hill, they used the old Northallerton police station on East Road as their headquarters. This proved most inadequate and a new building was constructed on the same site, seen here, in 1880. In January 1991 these police buildings were demolished and superseded by an open area.

A totally new police headquarters was ratified in 1907, backed by a North Riding County Council vote of 47–12, and was built adjacent to the County Hall on the south side of Racecourse Lane. The building was completed by Blacker Bros of Bramley, Leeds for £9,429 with occupation beginning on 1 May 1910. This building was highly popular with those who worked and lived there with its tall airy rooms and view over the cricket field and beyond. It is seen here in 1948.

OCCASIONS & EVENTS

An incredible series of simultaneous aeroplane accidents occurred early in the morning of Friday 15 May 1914 when six of the ten biplanes of No. 2 Squadron Royal Flying Corps, on a flight from Seaton Carew, crashed around Northallerton having flown into dense fog. There were two fatalities at Lovesome Hill but in this crash, photographed on the day of the accident, Lieutenant Rodwell, the pilot, and his companion, Air Mechanic William Lee, were unscathed although the former only had 20 ft visibility when he crash-landed half a mile from Danby Wiske railway station on Walter Todd's Lazenby Hall farm. Rodwell's badly damaged No. 332 BE biplane is surrounded by fascinated locals.

The Volunteer's Band is leading an extensive procession through a High Street decked with flags and bunting on the occasion of the Coronation of Edward VII in August 1902. It was a memorable day in Northallerton with a packed church service, Applegarth Sports, 1,000 children having tea in relays at the Town Hall and a brilliant firework display, the crowd stretching from the church wall back to the Town Hall.

A military escort for a deceased serviceman is seen here, possibly at the end of the First World War. His remains were returned to Northallerton by train, where they were retrieved by relatives and met by an escort party which accompanied the casket to the cemetery. Standing with heads bowed and arms reversed, this appears to be a Royal Air Force contingent and the dead man would in all probability be in that arm of the Services.

A Girl Guides' Rally was held in 1935 at Oak Mount, Thirsk Road and the Northallerton Guides are assembled with their leaders, Miss Hilda Russell and Miss Watson. Back row, left to right: Evelyn Bendelow, Nancy Leach, Peggy Walton, Edna Stubbs, Kitty Stockdale. Second row: Kathleen Smith, Vera Mathers, Vera Dawson, Edith Tweedy, May Sedgwick, Olive Wilson, -?-, Joan Wallis, Ethel Marshall, Janet Stokes, Miss Fawcett, Dorothy Ratcliffe. Third row: Joan Stubbs, -?-, Miss Hilda Russell, Miss Watson, (kneeling/sitting) Dorothy Dale, Betty Morris. Front row: Eva Shields, Kathy Eyre, Edna Fowler, Doris Stockdale, -?-, Doreen Hogg.

Thronged around the market cross on 28 January 1936 are a great array of people waiting to hear the Chairman of Northallerton Urban District Council, A. Howard, read the proclamation announcing Edward VIII as the new monarch. Imagine then the consternation in the crisis which led to the King's abdication, a situation in which the local MP, Thomas Dugdale, was much involved as Parliamentary Private Secretary to the Prime Minister, Stanley Baldwin.

The Society for the Establishment and Support of Sunday Schools was founded in 1785 and their 150th Anniversary was marked by the local Sunday Schools parading through the town in 1935. Passing here is the Baptist Sunday School contingent led by Mr Smith, the builder, and including sisters, Laura Foster and Doris Stubbs, Laura's children Marjorie and Gladys Foster (the latter, mother of the Severs brothers), Peggy Smithson, Annie Brown and Eric James who later became a Baptist minister and married Marjorie Foster.

A happy Zion Church Sunday School trip to Reeth in summer 1939 is captured here. Most of the smiling children have been identified: back row, left to right: Mrs Sims, -?-, Gladys Walker, -?-, -?-, Betty Kinchin, Revd Mr Sims, Florrie Butterfield. Second row: Eric Toft, Dorothy Gill, Ivy Coxall, Jean McKenna, Miss Walker. Third row: -?-, Mary Wilbor. Fourth row: Duggie Derbyshire, Tommy Wilbor, Gordon Toft, Miss Walker, George Hepplestone. Front row: Nellie Hepplestone, Elsie Coxall, Joan Wilbor, Mavis Toft, Keith Wilbor.

On Friday 1 March 1946 Northallerton was front page headline news in all the national daily papers because of a violent riot which had erupted the previous day in the 'Army Glasshouse' gaol housing Army offenders. Starting at 11 a.m., in no time a mass of damage had been done, fires started and windows shattered. Eventually seven ringleaders held the roof top (as seen on the photograph), hurling dismantled slates at anything below.

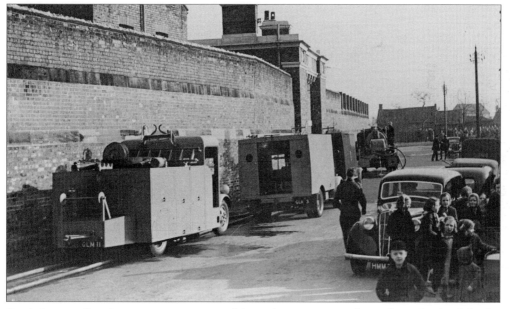

For their own safety the numerous spectators of the gaol riot were moved out of East Road and the fire engines assembled there began to play heavy jets of water relentlessly on the defiant roof-top prisoners. As darkness fell searchlights dramatically lit up the prison, and finally at 7.40 p.m. the seven recalcitrant prisoners surrendered.

In 1950 D Company (Northallerton) 5th Battalion Army Cadet Force, Green Howards won two trophies and this is the commemorative photograph. The Worsley Cup for Efficiency is held by Peter Beadle on the extreme right with Bill Roden slightly behind him and in the centre Eric Boddye has the Jackson Rose Bowl for Shooting flanked by Brian Close, left, and Les Hall, right. Seated, left to right, are Captain George Brown, Commanding Officer, Lieutenant Colonel C.N. Littleboy, County Commander and Major Bennett, Battalion Commander, with Sergeant Major Jack Jones standing on the left and Lieutenant Basil Young on the right. Other cadets are James Rowntree, extreme left, and on the back row, Ernest Common and Terance Halliday, third and second from the right.

Northallerton hosted this great British Legion Rally in 1950, the size of which can be gauged from the depth of the parade in front of the imposing Northallerton war memorial and the number of visiting buses in sight. Revd Frederick Baines, Vicar of Northallerton, led the open-air service and at the rear is trumpeter George Kelley who played the 'Last Post' and 'Reveille' before the Legion Branches paraded through the town.

The Girl Guides Northallerton Grammar School Company marched on the St George's Day Parade in 1951, from Northallerton Parish Church, down Friarage Street and past old buildings long-since demolished. They were watched en route by hundreds of spectators and the Guides looked particularly smart for the occasion, their outside rank behind Scouter George Hepplestone being: Doreen Smith, Dorothy Thompson, Jennifer Bensley, Lana Cockerill, Patricia Earnshaw and Chrstine Greer.

In February 1952 came another royal proclamation to announce the accession to the throne of Queen Elizabeth II. Schoolchildren are at the front of the gathering with many adults off camera when Arthur Skelton, Chairman of the Northallerton UDC, read the proclamation supported by councillors Ritchie Pick, A. Welsby, C.F. Atkinson, T. Jackson, Jack Swain and Tom Lightfoot.

So popular was this pub outing for Harewood Arms regulars to Scarborough in 1952 that two buses were filled. Some recognizable faces are Arthur Wilson (mine host) and brother Gordon Wilson, Harry Thompson snr and son Harry Thompson, Tom Sedgwick snr and sons Jack and Ernie Sedgwick, George Lee, Desmond Hill, Hugh Clark, Geoff Gill, Les Green, Joe Wilbor, R. Nelson, Sid Hatfield and Stan Abbott.

On the Armistice Day parade of November 1952 the Northallerton Army Cadet detachment passes the saluting base in mid-High Street, led by Under Officer Peter Beadle (who later became an RAF Volunteer Reserve Flight Lieutenant) and Warrant Officer Ernest Place, who eventually rose to the rank of Major in the Cadet Force. The Reviewing Officer on the dais is the Commanding Officer of Royal Air Force Leeming supported by the be-medalled Chairman of Northallerton UDC Geoffrey Wrigley, a leading Northallerton solicitor. Of final note are the shops and pubs which have long since gone.

Some of the most popular events in the local calendar were the Northallerton and District Young Farmers dances, one of which is seen here at Northallerton Town Hall in 1953. Unfortunately a mere photograph cannot convey the jollity, enjoyment, enthusiasm and companionship of the dances with everyone bent on making a good night of it. The 'Gay Gordons' and 'Lancers' danced with bucolic buoyancy had to be seen to be believed!

A notable visitor to Northallerton in 1944 was the Chief Guide, Lady Baden-Powell, who came to inspect the Brownies and Girl Guides. She is seen here with Hilda Russell, the Divisional Commandant, of Hatfield Road, talking to some of the younger girls in front of the Allertonshire School where the inspection took place.

The celebrations on Queen Elizabeth's Coronation Day at Northallerton in 1953 were undermined by incessant rain which is indicated in the photograph by both the sodden ground and the people garbed in raincoats. A mammoth planned procession, of which these vehicles were part, a 'bumper' bonfire in the Applegarth and dancing until midnight in the High Street were all cancelled. However, 1,600 children's coronation mugs were distributed and a most popular event was a Coronation Fayre at the Friarage Hospital.

The Northallerton branch of the Royal Air Force Association is assembled here on Remembrance Sunday, November 1955 in front of shops which are now among some of the affectionate names of the past: Vittys, Hancocks and G. Todd. From left to right are Sid Hepplestone, Tommy Place, Bernard Spence, -?-, -?-, -?-, -?-, Noel Smith, Bill Smith, Tommy Welton, Robbie Roberts, -?- behind, Geoff Wetherill, -?- behind, Alan Hepplestone, Denis Beadle, Philip Wooton, Harold Bartram (Standard Bearer), Wilf Kell, Charlie Trueman, Wally Smith, Arthur Hampton, John Wilson, Jeff Raistrick, Albert Winspear, Cliff Coldwell, Les Randall, -?-, Dave Smith, Alf Gunn, -?-, Johnny Briggs and Geoff Blair.

A 'Charm Contest' was organized in 1954 by Toc H in the Northallerton Town Hall and was judged by local personality Dr Doris Todd. The winners were Dorothy Thompson at the back with Christine Greer on the right; the two younger girls were Judy Mattison, to the rear, with Gillian Storm in front of her.

The Odd Fellows Arms, Northallerton was the venue for this meeting of the Richmondshire Constituency Labour Party in the mid-1950s. Back row, left to right: Derek Collins, Geoff Blair, Hilary Marquand (Labour Government Minister), -?-, Tom Brocklebank (North Riding County Councillor). Front row: -?-, Mrs Marquand, Gary Simons (Secretary), Mrs Simons, Mrs Earnshaw, Mrs Barraclough.

The annual dinner of the Northallerton Branch of the Green Howards' Association in 1958 at the Golden Lion. The top table featured, left to right: -?-, Mrs Forbes, Tom Riordan (author's father and President), Brigadier George Eden (Colonel of the Regiment), Major Tony Steede (Chairman), Mrs Faith Steede, Colonel Johnathan Forbes (Regimental Secretary), Mrs Esther Riordan (author's mother).

A visit made in 1952 by the now combined Northallerton and Dales Water Board and officials to the new reservoir under construction at Sheep Wash Valley, Osmotherley. This Cod Beck Reservoir was opened by Sir Thomas Dugdale, the Minister of Agriculture on Saturday 12 December 1953 by which time the original building estimate of £276,000 in 1949 had escalated to a cost of £564,070.

After years of fund-raising and controversy, a War Memorial to the fallen Northallerton heroes of the Second World War, in the form of the Memorial Swimming Baths, was opened on Bullamoor Road in June 1961. Lady Masham is seen at the microphone officially declaring the baths open, the service representatives are at the back with their standards and on the extreme right, wearing his chain of office, is Kenneth Hird, Chairman of Northallerton UDC. R.S. Mortimer was the architect and the main contractor Walter Thompsons Ltd.

The British Legion Club, Northallerton Committee 1958 answers a photo-call. Back row, left to right: Bill Sturgiss, Tom Bickerdyke, -?-, Harry Thompson jnr, H. Marshall, M. Robinson, Mr Gallen, L. Skelton, -?-, G. Lee Vincent. Front row: J. Smedley, R. Johnson, Dr Keith Balfour, William Robinson, Joe Smithers, Harry Thompson snr, Arthur Skelton.

Kellett and Pick were one of the most successful garage enterprises and motor traders in Northallerton and on this occasion in 1963 several of their main management team are assembled. Some of them are identified, left to right: -?-, Mike Phrizell, John Kellett, -?-, -?-, Fred Hanby, -?-, Olwyn Cockerill, Ron Lynas.

Group Captain Douglas Bader, the Second World War fighter pilot hero, who lost both his legs before the conflict, had long been connected with the North Riding Youth Club movement after first being involved by Lady Dugdale. He visited Northallerton in the summer of 1967 as co-patron of a North Riding Youth Rally which attracted over 5,000 people to the Applegarth. Douglas Bader is photographed inspecting the Northallerton Air Training Corps, accompanied by their Commanding Officer, Flight Lieutenant (VR) Peter Beadle.

DRAMATIC ART & MUSIC

A view from the Applegarth in 1956 of the once famous Theatre Royal, built in 1800 by actor, manager and impresario Samuel Butler, as one of a circuit of five theatres including the internationally acclaimed Georgian Theatre, Richmond. Butler moved with his acting troupe around the 'circuit', Northallerton's turn coming in the autumn to coincide with its popular Races and the famed St Bartholomew's Fair. The Theatre Royal was sold in 1834 to the Primitive Methodists who worshipped here until 1891.

THEATRE, NORTHALLERTON.

BY DESIRE,

AND UNDER THE IMMEDIATE PATRONAGE OF

Major Hartley

AND THE

OFFICERS

Of the North York Yeomanry Cavalry.

On Thursday, Sept. 27th, 1832,

Will be performed the admired Comedy, of

The Soldier's
Daughter

Governor Heartall	... Mr. BANKS
Frank Heartall	Mr. J. E. PARRY
Charles Woodley	Mr. RIDER
Mr. Malfort	Mr. SHIELDS
Ferret	Master BANKS
Timothy Quaint	Master L. BANKS
Simon	Mr. BOWES
Widow Cheerly	Mrs. J. E. PARRY
Mrs. Fidget	Mrs HARGRAVE
Mrs. Malfort	Mrs. BANKS
Susan	Mrs. COOPER

A COMIC SONG, BY MR. SHIELDS.
A FAVORITE SONG, BY MRS. BANKS.
A Comic Song, by Mr. Shields.

The whole to conclude with the laughable Farce, of the

Dead Shot.

Captain Cannon	Mr. BANKS
Mr. Timid	Mr. J. E. PARRY
Mr. Wiseman	Mr. SHIELDS
Frederick	Mr. COYLE
Bailiffs, &c.	Messrs. RIDER ANTHONY
Chatter	Mrs. BANKS
Louisa Lovetrick	Mrs. J. E. PARRY

Doors to open at seven, and begin at half-past.—Boxes, 3s.—Pit, 2s.—Gallery, 1s.
Mr Parry will feel obliged by the Trades-people allowing the Bills to be seen in their Windows.

LANGDALE, PRINTER, NORTHALLERTON.

The Theatre Royal was within months of closing when this performance took place in 1832 but it had seen halcyon days with many of the greatest contemporary actors and actresses treading its boards. The premier actor of his time, Edmund Kean, is said to have started his acting career here with a 'walk on' part. Stephen Kemble, another famous actor, played here and did not have to make up for Falstaff as he weighed thirty stone!

Seen just after its erection by Dan Oakley Limited in 1920 is the Central Cinema, the second cinema in Northallerton; the Cinema de Luxe had been built in 1913, down Romanby Road. Melbourne Yard was demolished to make way for the Central but the latter shared the same fate when a northern access road to the Applegarth car park was constructed in 1961/2. But by that time the Central had given forty years entertainment to generations of appreciative people, showing four films a week.

Amateur artistes, concert parties and vaudeville acts had their local heyday in the pre-television days of the first half of this century. One of these was the Primitive Methodist Church Concert Party photographed in the 1930s. Back row, left to right: Peggy Sykes, Fred Hutchinson, M. Espiner, Ken Farmery, Cecily Sturdy, Fred Morley, Kathy Sykes. Middle row: -?-, Eric Mason. Front row: Ruth Thompson, Fred Archer, Barbara Sykes.

This local dance band – the 'Elite Dance Band Northallerton' – was very popular especially in the years before the Second World War. It played at such venues as the Town Hall, Church House and Catholic Hall as well as numerous village halls. The instrumentalists were Harry Wetherill (drummer), Harry Wright (banjo), Anthony Liddell (violin) and Johnny Briggs (piano).

In the late 1930s the Church of England Concert Party re-enacted the 'Crowning of the May Queen' at the Church House and many of the cast are identifiable in this photograph. Back row, left to right: Joyce Garden, Revd George Duckworth (curate) -?-, -?-, Mr Hogg, Mary Robinson, Mr Hardisty, Miss Marshall, Miss Dawson, Olive Rooke, Doris Garden, Geoff Wetherill, Fred Bolland, Doris Robinson. Front row: Ruth Hawksby, Mahla Deighton, Vera Mather, Winnie Garden, Elsie Carr, Doreen Thompson, Frances Garden (May Queen), -?-, -?-, Joyce Morris, Elsie Foster, -?-.

An earlier Concert Party in 1930 called the 'Jolly Revellers', several members of which later joined the 'Jolly Boys' vaudeville troupe, which was very popular in the late 1930s. The 'Jolly Revellers' were, back row, left to right: Peggy Smithson, John Rooke, Eric James, Fanny Smith, George Hardisty. Front row: Gladys Foster, -?-, Jessie Smith, Marjorie Foster.

As part of the celebrations for the Festival of Britain in 1951, a magnificent 'Pageant in Six Scenes of the History of Northallerton' was performed by 300 local amateurs on the north side of the Church Green on the evenings of 18, 20 and 23 June. Hundreds watched the performances and this particular assembly shows the actors in the Battle of the Standard 1138, with Norman Bryning, headmaster of the Allertonshire School, in the centre wearing a square mitre, playing the English religious leader Ralph, the Bishop of Orkney. Mr Bryning is still active, hale and hearty, at ninety-six years of age.

Another Festival of Britain production was the play *Wives and Daughters* on 3, 4 and 5 May 1951 at the Allertonshire School. This comedy was well reviewed and attracted full and appreciative audiences. In this scene, left to right, are R. Foulkes, Nancy McDougle, Phyllis Elliott, Mary Wedderburn (sitting), Lloyd Dales, J. Springett. The Allertonshire Players, who produced the play, flourished for three decades in Northallerton, keeping up their excellent standards.

From 1946, for fifty successive years, Northallerton Amateur Variety Company have staged annual pantomimes which have captivated their sell-out audiences. *Aladdin*, presented in 1960, was one such example and some of the most redoubtable characters of the pantomimes of that era are shown here. Back row, left to right: Terence Naylor (Mustapha), Geoff Naylor (Tu Lo), Cec Richardson (Tu Hi). Front row: Lady Barwick (Producer), Joan Wetherill (Princess), Albert Gaskell (Emperor), Vina Galloway (Spirit of the Lamp).

Romanby Women's Institute drama team was very successful, especially in the 1950s and 1960s. In 1956 they won the Yorkshire Federation's Drama Competition with the play *Spinning Jenny*. Back row, left to right: Kathleen M'Cartney, Amy Boddye, Kathleen Bateson, Vivienne Snaith. Front row: Dorothy Finnely, Margaret Elliott (Producer), Dorothy Oldham.

Since 1909 Northallerton Grammar School scholars annually presented a well-received play, often of a Shakespearean character, as was the case with *A Midsummer Night's Dream* in 1950. Edwin Bush, the history master, produced the play and the cast can be identified as follows: back row, left to right: David Uttley, Mick Riordan (author), Bill Roden, Ernest Common, Sheena Wilson, Bob Bennison, Brenda Hartley (hidden), Roger Hartley, Paddy Tooley, Jean Dunlop, John Boynton, Eric Boddye, Bryan Raine. Front row: third left Catherine Wood, sixth from left Valerie Wilkinson.

The Girls' Friendly Society of Northallerton often gave entertainments and their company is assembled here in the mid-1950s. Back row, left to right: -?-, Jean Carter, Shirley Winspear, -?-, Lorna Ware, Marjorie Coxall. Middle row, standing: Jean Lewis, Margaret Wright, Dorothy Thompson, Sheila Wilbor, Doreen Castle, -?-, Kathleen Stockdale, -?-, Doreen Pearson. Front row, kneeling: Joan Richardson, Anne Pashby, Avril Morley, Marion Kendrew, Valerie Winspear, -?-, Anne Costick, Pat Candler, Marian Winn, Rene Stockdale, Morag Wilson.

Northallerton's third and most opulent cinema the Lyric, photographed here in 1960, was built by Walter Thompson and Son and opened on Saturday 28 October 1939 with the first film being *We're Going to be Rich*, starring Gracie Fields. The cinema, which was erected on the site of old property including Bowman's yard, held 700 seats which were often completely filled until the mid-1950s when television became more accessible.

After the Second World War the Lyric held a highly successful children's Matinée Club on Saturdays and here some members are included in a Christmas Fancy Dress competition on the cinema stage, in about 1947. Front row, left to right: Clive Dunning, Keith Severs, Blanche Smith, Dorothy Thompson, Morag Wilson, -?-, Ronnie Palliser, Peter Coulson, Roy Shyvers, Moira Clark, Shirley Winspear.

The Northallerton Amateur Operatic Company has been responsible for consistently outstanding annual operatic productions during the past five decades, playing to full houses at various venues, notably the Lyric Cinema and later the Hambleton Community Centre. Assembled are the full company of *Magyar Melody* in November 1966. Back row, left to right: David Carr, Michael Stone, -?-, Bill Williams, Maurice Cook, Alyn Armstrong, George Dobson, Robert Carr, Ray Barnett, Alyn Mitchinson, Brian Rawling, Anthony Logan, Don Charlton, Jack Wilson. Third row: Roger Hanson, Arthur Robson, Margaret Umpleby, Fred Shaw, Edith Stone, Bernard Hirst, Shirley Atkinson, Derek Turner, Eva Blamires, John Common, Chris Hird, Pauline Hanson, Len Minton, Patricia Peacock, -?-, Eileen Hird, Bert Whittaker, Dorothy Clark, 'Nobby' Clark, Mary Davis, Tom Umpleby. Second row: Irene Morton, Betty Cooper, Margaret Ellis, Anne Glasper, Renee Simpson, Jennifer Storm, Elsa Clark, Joanne Walker, Anne Smith, Mary Evans, -?-, Millie Woods, -?-, Midge Common. Front row: Judith Andrew, -?-, Sally Penman, Audrey Turnbull, Doreen Monk, Barbara Ellis, Gillian Logan, Margaret Swall, Sue Poppleton, Christine Williamson, J.S. Tweddle -?-, -?-.

Northallerton Choral Society
with the choirs of
Easingwold and Thirsk

present

HANDEL'S
"MESSIAH"

in the

TOWN HALL

TUESDAY, 9th DECEMBER, 1958.

AT 7-15 P.M.

Soloists :

ADA ALSOP	..	..	SOPRANO
EUNICE MOORE	..	..	CONTRALTO
EDWARD YORKE	..	..	TENOR
EUGENE BUSFIELD	..		BASS
RONALD WILD	..	..	TRUMPET

ORCHESTRA :
Leader : CLIFFORD J. WALKER
Continuo : SEFTON COTTOM

Conductor :
A. MATTINSON WILSON

PROGRAMME 6d.

The National Federation of Music Societies to which this Society is affiliated supports this performance with funds provided by the Arts Council of Great Britain.

Works previously performed by the Society :

Christmas Oratorio	..	..	.. *Bach*
Sleeper Wake—Cantata		..	.. *Bach*
Bide with us	..	..	.. *Bach*
Peasant Cantata	..	..	.. *Bach*
Begin the Song—Cantata		..	.. *Blow*
Acis and Galatea	..	..	.. *Handel*
Coronation Anthems	..		.. *Handel*
The Messiah	..	..	.. *Handel*
The Creation	..	..	.. *Haydn*
The Passion	..	..	.. *Haydn*
Elijah	..	..	.. *Mendelssohn*
Psalm 86	..	..	.. *Holst*
Psalm 148	..	..	.. *Holst*
Three Songs of Courage		..	.. *Dyson*
Fantasia on Xmas Carols		..	.. *V. Williams*
Benedicite	..	..	.. *V. Williams*
Thanksgiving for Victory		..	.. *V. Williams*
Psalm 150	..	..	.. *V. Williams*
Songs of the Bavarian Highlands		..	.. *Elgar*
Concert Versions of Opera :—			..
" Carmen "	..	..	.. *Bizet*
" Tom Jones "	..	..	.. *German*
" Merrie England "	..	..	.. *German*
16th and 17th Madrigals, etc.			
The Bartered Bride		..	.. *Smetana*
Requiem Mass	..	..	.. *Mozart*
Imperial Mass	..	..	.. *Haydn*
Soirèes Musicale	..	..	.. *Rossini-Britten*

This rendering of the *Messiah* in December 1958 was only one of a series of virtuoso performances by the Northallerton Choral Society from the 1940s to the 1960s. The choir was conducted brilliantly by A. Mattinson (Gerry) Wilson while the leader of the orchestra was the multi-talented Clifford Walker, who started his musical career in a quartet which included John Barbirolli. Gerry was also the mercurial choirmaster of the Northallerton Parish Church Choir, his memory now celebrated by the annual award of the Gerry Wilson Cup for the most outstanding chorister.

SCHOOLDAYS

These eight children and the teacher comprise the whole of Deighton School in 1910. Lawrence Newcombe is standing at the back, second on the left. This historic photograph was one of several supplied by Doreen Newcombe (née Forth).

An interesting and rare photograph of Northallerton Grammar School in 1931 shows the Girls' Senior
Hockey team. Back row, left to right: Miss D. Jackson, Dorothy Harland, Marjorie Verrill, May East,
Margaret Steel, Joyce Brand, Eileen Bennett, G. Wray (Groundsman). Front row: Frances Garden,
Minnie Thompson, Florence Aconley, Gladys Naisbitt, Vina Sherwin, Grace Gibson. It is noted that all
the young ladies wore pads – was the game tougher then or were they just more protected?

The intriguing thing about this picture of Northallerton Grammar School Form VA in 1931 is the low
number of only eleven students and the fact that they all came from villages outside the town. This was in
the days of 'fee paying' with few scholarships. Back row, left to right: Richard Hebron (Burneston), John
Sturdy (South Otterington) Mr K. Whatnough (form master), John Broadway (Thornton-le-Moor –
killed in war) John Bell (Brompton). Middle row: Ellen Shepherd (Appleton Wiske), Miriam Edwards
(Pickhill). Front row: Eileen Bennett (Great Smeaton), Eva Culley (Brompton), Gladys Naisbitt (North
Otterington), Una Sherwin (Bedale).

Brompton Methodist Sunday School, *c.* 1938. Back row, left to right: Dorothy Blair, Maurice Hardcastle, Frances Robinson, Eileen Dunn, Frances Nixon, Raymond Richardson, Richard Blair, Alan Hodgson, Denis Hutchinson, Mabel Robinson, Minister's wife, Mabel Peacock. Second row: Mr Cansfield, Margaret Blair, Wilf Hardcastle, Freda Oxendale, Raymond Nixon, Edith Easton, Nora Dunn, Gladys Dowson, Beatrice Robinson, Nora Peacock, Harwood Peacock. Third row: John Blair, Leslie Walker, Norman Willis, Kenneth Walker, John Stainthorpe, Peter Ward, Norman Burn. Fourth row: Lewelyn and Theodore Hooper, Stan Hardcastle, Stan Dunn, Ted Tyreman, Muriel Johnson, Brenda Bell, Joyce Barnforth, Ada Ford, Ruth Hutchinson. Fifth row: -?-, Margaret Nixon, Sonia Burn, Mavis Richardson, June Barker, Vera Frost, Brenda Brown, Winnie Bellwood, Violet Britain, Miss Thackeray, Doreen Brown, Dora Robinson, Peggy Brown. Front row: Tommy Thackeray, Wilf Robinson, Stan Shepherd, Brian Burn, Colin Burn, Stan Sawdon, Leslie Randell, Geoff Forth, Joe Robinson.

Photographed from Brompton Road in 1946, the Allertonshire County Modern School took its first intake of pupils in September 1941 having been built to the design of the London architects Scott, Shepherd and Breakwell who had previously been responsible for the Shakespeare Memorial Theatre at Stratford-upon-Avon. The school was experimental and very much ahead of its times – the brainchild of Frank Barraclough, the North Riding's brilliant Secretary of Education, who lived at Thirsk Road, Northallerton.

The senior class at East Road School, 1949–50. Back row, left to right: Roy Shyvers, Neil Hayward, David Cation, Derek Clarke, Barry Joyce, Alan Ramsden, Neville Shaw, Trevor Freer, John Winspear, Alan Robinson, Bernard Bradley. Second row: Miss Amy Lumley, Alan Moss, Sheila Postgate, Marjorie Clark, Shirley Bishton, Marjorie Hutton, Pat Briggs, Doris Place, Barbara Wilson, Mavis Smart, Joyce Gibson, Pat Guy, Keith Severs. Third row: Georgina Burns, Pat Sherwood, Morag Wilson, Margaret Weighell, Sheila Sturdy, Suzanne Rider, Rita Baty, Pat Hind, Kathleen Neesam, Dorothy Thompson, Doreen Pearson, Margaret Smith. Front row: -?-, Geoffrey Clemmit, Ronnie Palliser, Tommy Adams, Michael Worth, David Richardson, Derek Hartley.

Northallerton Grammar School, pictured in 1946, is still showing the signs of wartime with the air-raid shelters prominent in the foreground. Fortunately they were only used for practice. Since the opening of the school in 1909 the student roll had increased greatly and extensions eventually became necessary. In 1939 Dan Oakley built a new library and gymnasium for £6,600, the latter being the tall building on the extreme right of the photograph.

Northallerton Grammar School, form 3A, in 1948. Back row, left to right: Ken Robson, Colin Nicholson, James Sedgewick, Donald Richardson, Robin Reed, Harold Bennison, Mervyn King. Middle row: Shirley Neesham, Eileen Tempest, Margaret Thompson, Brenda Hartley, June Miller, Mary Snow, Winifred Fall, Louie Coates. Front row: Dorothy Garlick, Catherine Wood, Shirley Wilkinson, Isabell Fall, Miriam Charles, Mr Edwin Bush (form master), Eileen Janney, Winnie I'anson, Helen Dales, Doreen Forth, Dorothy Holmes.

Northallerton Grammar School produced *Tobias and the Angel* in March 1948 and this is a scene from the play. The Bandit (Brian Glasper) threatens Tobias (Mick Riordan) who is 'sore afraid', but the calm Angel (Judy Bailey) is completely unperturbed by this merely human disturbance. This was the zenith of the two boys' thespian attainments, but Judy went on to be a professional actress with Bristol Repertory Company and made several appearances on BBC TV and Radio.

These cheerful children are involved in the East Road School Sports Day on Applegarth, *c.* 1937. Back row, left to right: B. Gilbank, H. Gill, ? Hatfield, ? Durham ? Brough, Alistaire Carter, J. Kelley, Fred Coxall. Second row: Ernie Sedgwick, Muriel Fisburn, -?-. Third row: Kitty Alderson, Eva Taylor, George Kelley, Molly Wright. Front row: May Sedgwick, Hilda Coxall, Ivy Coxall, Doris Coxall.

Industrious work goes on at the Applegarth School in 1938, the contentment of the scene contrasting strongly with the tragic events of the Second World War soon to come which caused great consternation. The sinking of HMS *Hood* in 1941, the children's 'adopted' ship, with the loss of all the crew except three, had a traumatic effect on many of the pupils, as did the Halifax plane crash which narrowly missed the school, engulfing the windows in smoke and fire on 2 December 1943. The seven airmen in the Halifax bomber were killed and over 1,300 people perished in the *Hood*. Poignantly, many of the sailors carried with them the *Hood*'s Prayer, composed by the Applegarth School which ended: 'Make me strong of heart and fearless in danger and whether I live or die, keep me in thy Almighty keeping.'

The Northallerton Grammar School tennis team of 1950 was, back row, left to right: Clara Grainger, Rhoda Chapman, Dorothy Holmes. Front row: Dorothy Hall, Hazel Brown, Brenda Hartley.

This smart class at the Allertonshire in 1953 is Form 4A. Back row, left to right: Sid Adams, G. Dinsdale, D. Dillon, J. Christian, David Lindop, A. Saunders, David Cromoty, D. Wilkinson, L. Doy, E. Spence. Middle row: W. Cornforth, Jean Macintosh, G. Sissons, R. Mowbray, K. Coates, David Brown, D. Carr, E. Godfry, J. Harland, E. Castle. Front row: A. Charlton, C. Lowes, J. Taylor, E. Gladwin, M. Clark, Mrs D. Young, M. Lowther, J. Hay, M. Foster, J. Bloomfield, Minnie Lakin.

Northallerton Grammar School Hockey XI, 1950. Back row, left to right: Brenda Hartley, Margaret Thompson, Helen Dales, Vivienne Taylor, Catherine Wood, Jean Clark, Winifred Fall. Front row: Jean Ellwood, Sheila Clegg, Catherine Staples, Doris Crooks, Winnie I'anson. There were five North Riding County Schools players in the team.

Northallerton Grammar School Football XI, 1952. This was the most successful football team at the school for several years. Back row, left to right: John DiPalma, George Atkinson, David Simpson, John Sheehan, Peter Grainger, Bob Bennison, John Scott. Front row: Mervyn King, Charles Brown, Brian Glasper, Mick Riordan, Roger Hartley.

Northallerton Grammar School cricket squad, 1950. For three seasons, from 1949 to 1951, Northallerton Grammar School cricket eleven was unbeaten and this was the team in the second year of their achievement. Back row, left to right: Colin Nicholson (scorer), Vernon Tennant, Christopher Greensit, Donald Richardson, Bill Roden, Bob Bennison, Brian Glasper, Mervyn King. Front row, seated: Arthur Arrand (cricket master), Roger Hartley, Eric Boddye, Sean Crawford, Harry Brown, Mick Riordan, Arthur T. Richardson (headmaster). Crosslegged in front: Ernold Cuthbert, Douglas Metcalfe.

This well-turned-out form is C3 at the Allertonshire School in September 1950. Back row, left to right: George Riordan (author's younger brother), Raymond Brown, Kenneth Gaines, Gordon Grainger, Alan Ward, Tony Oldfield, Terence Meynell, Albert Pattison, David Kingsley, Denis Burn, Billy Stockdale, Colin Woodburn. Second row: Sylvia Barnett, Denise Watts, Una Christon, Mary Verity, Jenny Wood, Brenda Greenwood, Mercy Barlow, Anne Christon, Marjorie Watson, Maureen Greenbank. Front row, seated: Enid Wright, Nellie King, L. Turnbull, E. Feasby, Mr Fred Endersby, Audrey Smith, Barbara Wade, Grace Hind, Maureen Kirkbride. Crosslegged at the front: Keith Wells, Dick Ayling, Douglas Hodgson, Harold Brown, David Wright, Graham Turner.

Seen here are the Fifth Form boys of Northallerton Grammar School in 1950. When they came to the school in September 1945 they were, with their female classmates, the first group of pupils ever to enter the school having passed the 11+ examination. Back row, left to right: Brian Raine, Edward Kay, Harry Brown, Les Wheatley, Les Hall, Mike Metcalfe, Lou Randall, Vernon Tennant, Len Scott. Front row: John Boynton, Ray Hugill, Ernest Common, Mick Riordan, Maurice Macintosh, Brian Glasper, William Cooper.

Northallerton Grammar School, Form 4A, in 1955 includes Dorothy Thompson (now Mrs Young) who supplied this and several other photographs. Back row, left to right: John Wood, David Richardson, Michael Worth, Alan Ramsden, Frank Marshall, Michael Coulthard, -?-, Kenneth Hugill, Roy Shyvers. Middle row: Joan Little, Marjorie Smith, Keith Hardisty, John Shoemake, Keith Severs, Tony Rider, Neil Hayward, Martin Dennison, Joyce Whitfield, Margaret Smith. Front row: Pat Blair, Marjorie Hutton, Pat Briggs, Pat Sherwood, Joan Kirby, Mr Arthur Arrand, Barbara Watson, -?-, Pam Johnson, Judith Watson, Dorothy Thompson. Mr Arrand, the senior French master, was the form master.

The staff of Northallerton Grammar School assembled in 1955. This group contains many household names recalled by generations of ex-pupils. Back row, left to right: Miss Hardy, Isobel Telford, Bill Lowther, Mr Winter, Reg Welburn, Denis Woods, Jimmy Addison, Margaret Hobday, Shirley Law. Front row: Miss Alderson, Jack Clark, Miss Richardson, Arthur Arrand, Arthur T. Richardson (headmaster), Laura Webster (senior mistress), Robert Robson, Molly Telford, Charles Harper.

The Northallerton Grammar School tennis team of 1958. Back row, left to right: Sheila Adams, Angela Sladden, Alison Holmes. Front row: Dorothy Thompson, Joan Phizacklea, Joyce Whitfield.

The Guides were very popular in the Northallerton area in the 1940s and '50s and here is an informal view of the Northallerton Grammar School Guides Company in 1953. Left to right: Paddy Earnshaw, Dilys Ward, Brenda Shafto, Pat Hutton, Dorothy Thompson, Barbara Nelson (partly hidden) and Joan Little.

To end this schools section are the Northallerton Grammar School Hockey Team of 1957–8 posing against Grammar School Lane as a background. Back row, left to right: Angela Sladden, Anne Kirby, Elizabeth Webster, June Teasdale, Sheila Adams, Christine Shepherd, Pat Richardson (goal). Front row: Dorothy Thompson, Joan Phizacklea, Pat Briggs, Joyce Whitfield, Joan Crooks.

SPORTING PRINTS

*This is one of the earliest photographs known of a Northallerton Football League team and it shows the
Northallerton Thistles FC in about 1894 when they played in the Richmondshire League. Their
Headquarters were in the Railway Inn (now the Tap and Spile) North End and their pitch directly behind.
When they beat Northallerton there, 2–0, in 1894, 1,000 spectators watched. In the photograph Render,
the goalkeeper, is third from the right at the back and Bob Coverdale, the captain, is on the extreme right.
Other well-known players featured are Thomas Castle (left back), Bill Castle, A. Lee (half back),
W. Anderson (centre forward), A. Crowe (right wing) and A. Marshall (left wing).*

Northallerton Alliance FC were the main Northallerton football team before the Second World War, changing their name to Northallerton Town FC in 1952 forming the present club which is in the Northern League. Northallerton Alliance are seen here in 1939 and some of the individuals pictured are, back row, left to right: W. Bolland (third), Mick Hogg (fourth, leaning forward), Bob Pattinson (fifth, goalkeeper), Charlie Smith (seventh left), Alf Severs (eighth left). Front row: Stan Norwood, (first left), 'Sonny' Moody (third) and Denys Cooper (fourth left). All of these men were real stalwarts on the local postwar football scene.

Northallerton Cricket Club 1st XI assemble behind the York Senior League trophy which they won in 1948, playing on the County Hall cricket ground where this photograph was taken. Back row, left to right: John Camburn, Bill Catchpole, Ron Diggle, Walter Couling, Sam Wilkinson, Harry Render, Derek Fowler. Front row: Bill Howarth, Denys Cooper, Bill Pedley (captain), Harry Brown, Frank Lowther.

On Sunday 24 July 1949 Northallerton Cricket Club officially opened their new ground at the end of Farndale Avenue off Boroughbridge Road. Two club stalwarts, Bill Lowther (left) and Harry Render (right), conducted the opening ceremony by symbolically bowling a ball (Harry) and striking it with a bat (Bill) in front of the old Pagoda Pavilion which had been brought from the old field.

Northallerton Juniors won the Milbank Junior Cup in 1950 and are photographed with the trophy in the Applegarth. Back row, left to right: David Simpson, Brian Glasper, Mike Metcalfe, Mick Riordan, Peter Dodsworth, Brian Sedgwick. Front row: Kingsley Holden, Fred Nicholson, Keith Wilbor, Ron Holden, John DiPalma.

In an exciting final watched by several hundred people in July 1951, Northallerton Colts (average age seventeen) beat the very experienced North Riding NALGO side in the last over to win the Granindon Cup – Northallerton CC's knock-out trophy competed for by many local teams. The Colts team was, back row, left to right: Helen Dales (scorer), Keith Wilbor, Peter Nattress, Brian Sedgwick, John Palmer, Vernon Tennant, John DiPalma, Bill Taylor (umpire). Front row: Harry Brown, Don Johnson, Ken Palmer (captain), Mick Riordan, Brian Glasper. Bill Taylor was one of the area's finest sportsmen.

The Northallerton Town team of 1952–3, who beat Hawes in the Dales Cup semi-final. Back row, left to right: Ken Harrison, Ted Stevenson, Denys Cooper, Jack Stockdale, Ron Bateson, Fred Castle. Front row: Keith Wilbor, Tommy Pearson, Stan Schofield, Tommy Ford, Brian Glasper.

North Riding NALGO, whose players all worked at Northallerton, won the Shields Cup – inter-NALGO in Yorkshire – on 17 July 1952. Standing, left to right: W. Glue (umpire) K. Sawyer, A. Pearson, L. Spence, R. Fawcett, H. Brown, F. Cowell (scorer), G. Musgrave (umpire). Seated: F. Lowther, J. Broadley, W. Couling, Denys Cooper (captain), K. Jones, G. Harrison.

An early picture of Northallerton Spartans FC in 1955 showing their original team. The Spartans remained one of the most successful clubs in the local area both in the football and social spheres for forty years. Back row, left to right: Ken Norman, John DiPalma, Brian Sedgwick, David Simpson, Brian Glasper, Maurice Macintosh. Front row: Kingsley Holden, Pat Milner, Don Cranston, Mick Riordan, Pete Sawdon.

Albert Gaskell, Northallerton's first-class county umpire, is here officiating in the late 1950s at the famous Boxing Day Charity match at Allwoodley near Leeds, where many cricketing stars took part. Here, with Albert in between them, Don Wilson (Yorkshire) is bowling, while Brian Close (Yorkshire and England) is the non-striking batsman. Albert would have probably commented – 'a rose between two thorns'!

Taken in the 1954–5 season, this Northallerton Town team shows several changes to the side of 1952–3 mainly because of retirements from the game. It is especially notable because three Woodward brothers, hailing from Reeth, were all in the side together. Back row, left to right: Fred Castle, Ken Harrison, Brian Sedgwick, Ernie Woodward, Ron Bateson, Jimmy Woodward. Front row: Keith Wilbor, Derek Smales, David Woodward, Mick Riordan, Derek Fawcett.

In 1952 Northallerton CC repeated their 1948 feat of gaining the York Senior League Championship. This was mainly achieved by blending youth with experience, a tactic very much favoured by Bill Pedley, the Northallerton skipper. Back row, left to right: Tommy Rider, Frank Lowther, Alan Herbert, Ken Jones, Harry Brown jnr, Mick Riordan, Bill Taylor (umpire). Front row: Ray Fawcett, Harry Brown snr, Bill Pedley, Denys Cooper, Harry Render. The young players Doug Metcalfe, John Palmer, Brian Glasper and Vernon Tennant also played regularly.

Quoits was a very popular game in the Northallerton area and there were about eight teams that competed against one another. The Liberal Club was one such team, seen here in 1956, in the north eastern corner of the Applegarth in front of Sedgwick's House. Back row, left to right: Peter Dodsworth, T. King, John Carr, Jack Stockdale, Jim Dale. Front row: J. Durham, J. Davis, Alf Severs, S. Mullin, Stan Norwood, Ken Robson. The Northallerton and District Quoits League disbanded in 1963.

Yorkshire County Cricket Club often played in friendly matches with Northallerton and on 21 April 1956 they brought a strong side to face a Northallerton XI. In the Yorkshire ranks was a young 'Dicky Bird' destined to be a world-famous umpire. The Yorkshire team easily won the match. Back row, left to right: Jimmy Binks, ? Handley, Roy Booth, Ron Appleyard, Fred Trueman, Brian Bolus. Front row: Mick Cowan, Harold Bird, Willie Watson, Vic Wilson (captain), ? Slingsby.

Northallerton CC 2nd XI, who played in the Vale of Mowbray League to good effect, are photographed here in 1949. They were no mean cricketers and the team was abrim with 'characters', some almost legends in their own time. Whenever this team played there was never a dull moment. Back row, left to right: Jack Gill (umpire), Brian Dawson, Tom Riordan (author's eldest brother), John Hill, Bill Nelson, Alan Pearson, Bob Elgie, Henry Bendelow, Norman Read. Front row: Albert Gaskell, -?-, Ken Palmer (captain), Cliff Lightfoot, Jim Brandley.

Northallerton Town Juniors, who won the Milbank Junior Cup 1957–8, contained several players who became the backbone of local clubs in the next decade. Back row, left to right: Dave Robinson, Peter Wilbor, George Gill, Allan Martin, Colin Dunford, Mike Crawford, Cyril Swindon, Tony Rider. Front row: Lawrence Bayliss, Granville Fawcett, Tony Tennant, Antony Douglas, Tommy Lee.

Village cricket has been at the heart of local sport for 200 years and latterly the Northallerton Evening Cricket League has been highly successful and competitive. In 1960 Brompton won the title and played the rest of the League. Their team was, back row, left to right: B. Ripley (S. Otterington), Ernie Smith (Ainderby), J. Musgrove (S. Kilvington), Dick Marlsbury (Northallerton III), A. Middlemiss (Danby Wiske), Derek Fawcett (Combined XI). Front row: -?-, -?-, Bob Bell (Thornton-le-Moor), J. Hunter (Thornton-le-Moor), Mike Cowton (Leake).

Northallerton Spartans FC held their annual dinner of 1956 at the Golden Lion Hotel and assembled are their players and patrons consisting of many of Northallerton's best-known sports people. At the table, left to right: Harry Glasper (chairman), Anne Glasper, Albert Smales, Mrs Smales (President), Arthur and Mrs Arrand. Back row: Ken Christon, Brian Sedgwick, John DiPalma, Ken Palmer, Harold Bartram, Don Wood, Tom Almond, John Coverdale, Arthur Coverdale. Middle row: Ernie Smith, Doug Metcalfe, Pete Bateson, John Palmer, Dick Fletcher, Jim Macintosh, Brian Kendrew (half-hidden), Mike Simpkin, John Walker, Barry Joyce, Bill Johnson, Keith Severs, Maurice Macintosh, Derek Smales, George Johnson, Val Butterworth, Vicky Harrison, Des Hill, Mrs Kyle, Don Cranston, Cec Kyle.

Having commenced the Sports Section with the oldest team – Northallerton Thistles – it is appropriate to end it with the youngest. This is East Road School 1967–8 winners of the Northallerton and Brompton Junior Schools Cup. Back row, left to right: Danny Grainger, Brian Simpson, Jeremy Rocks, Steve Manning, Geoff Young, Mike Smalley, John Furness. Front row: Chris Wayman, Martin Blagden, Maurice Calvert, Steven Carey, Terence Espiner. But time waits for no man, and all of these have now hung up their boots!

AROUND THE TOWN

This postcard was sent by Joseph Burn from Brompton on 11 March 1906 to his aunt, Mrs Batt, at Frizinghall, Bradford. It is most unusual because Joseph himself is the sole person on the postcard as he points out. Interesting too are the large houses with garden extensions, the cobbled street and the Corn Exchange building in the distance.

A horse brake has brought these Brompton worthies to Byland Abbey, some ruins being seen in the background, in August 1903. The dress is of interest – probably Sunday-best with hats to the fore.

Water End, Brompton in mighty flood early in the century. Featured on the right is a resolute bullock pulling a cart bearing an equally indomitable Bromptonian, determined to reach his destination!

Brompton FC of 1950–1 are generally recognized as probably the best local team since the Second World War. Their excellent side won every trophy available and was one of all-round strength which included two players who had played professional football (Maurice Tooke and Sid Weighell) and some who could have, like Maurice Wetherill. Back row, left to right: 'Danny' Kay, D. Grimston, Cec Marchant, W. Hodgson, Derek Kendrew, Les Wetherill, H. Wetherill. Front row: Ken Baker, Maurice Tooke, Maurice Wetherill, Sid Weighell, Alf Marchant.

Brompton Whitsuntide Carnival and Sports has always been popular and the apogee of the village's year. Here in 1965 Miss Whitsuntide is being drawn through the crowded village by a handsome shire-horse – photographed by Ernest Satchell. Visitors used to swarm to the Carnival by train (especially from Hartlepool) but the loss of the railway has been offset by the motor vehicle and in 1965 attendances surpassed those of the pre-war period.

This view of Romanby Green, seen by two small boys in about 1900, has been similar for centuries with the western road leading to Yafforth passing over the ancient Packhorse Bridge on the edge of the village. Romanby House is visible at the road's end, for long the residence of Captain Thomas Hill, the North Riding's Chief Constable and where his son Alan Hill VC was brought up.

Romanby CC in 1927 at their ground, the Cherry Garth – now built over – in the village. Back row, left to right: Fred Cornforth, Billie Appleton, Arthur Stevenson, Mr Hibbard, Mike Hogg, John Hayward, John Wallace. Front row: Nin Smith, Herbert Carter, Charlie Moore, Joe Todd, Lawrie Gains, Stan Bainbridge, Mr Cranston, Fred Thompson.

This quaint and appealing winter scene at Ainderby on the main Northallerton road in about 1895 was certainly before the motor car! Ainderby School is on the left, St Helen's Church on the right and the Wellington Heifer public house ahead. But it is the horse and trap, the bicycle resting on the church wall and the couple strolling down the middle of the main road which catch the eye and imagination – it is the rare sight of a world gone by.

Bedale Grammar School is seen on the left of this 1900 postcard. It closed in 1935 because of a lack of pupils, many having elected to attend the revived and rebuilt Northallerton Grammar School. Bedale Grammar School has had a long history. In 1548 it and Northallerton Grammar School were ordered to be inspected by the King's Commissioners, Sir Walter Myldemaye and Robert Keylway, who gave both the schools satisfactory reports.

Bedale Police House depicted in a very old photograph – probably from about 1880. The horse and trap is particularly interesting because this was the first vehicle used by the North Riding Constabulary, the Chief Constable Thomas Hill purchasing sixteen such conveyances in 1857. In the 1890s the police were issued with bicycles, then motor bikes with sidecars and finally motor cars.

Ivy Godman, the wife of Air Commodore Arthur Godman of Great Smeaton Manor, in 1925. From 1876 the Godman family had been great benefactors to Great Smeaton and the North Riding, with Ivy no exception. She became North Riding Commandant of the Red Cross and was deeply involved in Great Smeaton affairs especially with the Women's Institute. When her husband died in the 1950s she sold Smeaton Manor as there was no heir, her son Captain Peter Godman having been killed at Dunkirk.

One hundred years of embroidery was celebrated by an exhibition in Great Smeaton village hall in May 1994 which featured a splendid set of thirty-two curtains embroidered by Great Smeaton's Women's Institute in 1930–1. Ivy Godman, a redoubtable needlewoman, completed one of the curtains; her mother-in-law, Ada Godman, had started the village's strong embroidery tradition in the 1880s. As seen in the example each curtain had the name of its needlewoman worked upon it – in this case that of Ivy Godman.

This postcard captures picturesque Great Smeaton Green complete with a tranquil horse, East House on the right and the village church in the background, c. 1910. The latter is the only church in the country dedicated to St Eloy, the patron saint of blacksmiths. The last Great Smeaton blacksmiths were the Fawcetts. St Eloy's was originally of Early English style and was last renovated in 1862.

Seen here in about 1920, Smeaton Manor was built in 1876–7 by the famous architect Phillip Webb for Major Arthur Godman. The Manor was constructed entirely of bricks made on the estate, the ensuing cavity being turned into a lake, and the entire building cost £6,500. Tall, stately and erected externally and internally, in a local vernacular, Webb considered this to be one of his finest buildings and it was much copied by other architects.

This view of Catterick Bridge goes back to the beginning of this century when the population was around 650. The village is well known for its Roman connections. It was a key Roman town, *Caractacorum*, in the Roman defence system and on the great Roman road of North Ermine Street. St Anne's Parish Church tower is visible, the church having been rebuilt in 1412. The first Sunday School in England is attributed to Catterick in 1763.

Shooting has always been a leading pastime in the vicinity of Northallerton, on the moors, estates and farm-land. A fascinating tableau of a shooting party at Deighton Manor in about 1910 is presented here. In the group are John Emmerson (landlord of Deighton Moor) Dr Hutchinson (Northallerton), Mr Cook (Deighton Manor agent), Biggins Emmerson (gamekeeper), Mr Finch (general handyman), and Johnson Toase (general labourer).

Sion Hill Hall, photographed in the 1930s, was erected in 1913 on the site of an old country house from 1760 owned by the Lascelles near Kirby Wiske. Walter Brierley of York, who was the architect, had Sion Hall built to a very high standard in a neo-Georgian style. Currently the Herbert Mawer Collection and Great Smeaton Women's Institute curtains (1931) are displayed here.

Leeming Bar School is assembled in 1930 and two families were earmarked by the donor Lou Dale. The Banks family – Brian (first left, third row), Kenneth (next left, author's brother-in-law) and Betty (in blazer, seventh right, third row); and the Beck boys, kneeling, first row; Fred (fifth left), who was killed at El Alamein with the Green Howards and Jim (extreme right), killed flying as a Navigator with Bomber Command.

This cricketing tableau from about 1900 is set on Newton House's cricket field which is now part of Royal Air Force, Leeming. William D. Russell, Newton House's proprietor, attracted superb teams to his home and also to Northallerton CC where he was the President. For example, he persuaded his close friend, the legendary Lord Hawke, to bring a full Yorkshire County side including George Hirst and Wilfred Rhodes to play Northallerton in 1902, 1903 and 1904.

St Peter's Church, Osmotherley is seen in this late nineteenth-century postcard. It was originally Norman, although evidence of an earlier Saxon church was discovered during its renovation in 1892. Osmotherley had the deserved reputation as a religious centre, also boasting a Roman Catholic chapel, a Friends' Meeting House, a Primitive Methodist chapel and an old Methodist chapel. Indeed, Osmotherley was one of John Wesley's favourite visiting places.

Scruton Manor dates back to at least the Domesday Book (1086) and there were halls on the site until this one was constructed in about 1640. It is featured here in 1900 on one of the several fine postcards supplied by Ken Wilson. Its most illustrious inhabitant was Roger Gale, Northallerton MP in 1705, 1707, 1708 and 1710 and the first Treasurer of the British Society of Antiquaries. Despite its grand past, however, it fell into disrepair and was demolished in the 1970s.

South Otterington Cricket Club won the Northallerton and District Cricket League in 1920 and 1923. Here they are in 1923 although some names could not be recalled. Back row, left to right: J. Pearson, Tom Smith, Bill Smith, J. Akers, -?-, -?-, Mr Atkinson, J. Appleton. Seated: -? , J. Wilson, Revd Mr Naylor, -?-, H. Appleton, -?-. Front row: -?-, -?-.

This successful and powerful South Otterington team won the Northallerton and District Evening League in 1953. Back row, left to right: L. Appleton, B. Ripley, A. Durham, W. Smith, K. Chapman, H. Bartram, M. Horner, H. Dixey, S. Pearson, G. Durham. Front row: H. Appleton jnr, T. Smith, G. Bartram, Miss M. Furness (president), H. Appleton snr, M. Chapman, W. Smart. It is said that some beds were not required that night as some victorious heroes preferred the hedgerows! And on this convivial note, it would seem appropriate to conclude with Giles Mornington's praise of Northallerton ale in 1697:

> 'Northallerton in Yorkshire does excel
> All England, Nay all Europe
> For strong ale.'

BRITAIN IN OLD PHOTOGRAPHS

To order any of these titles please telephone our distributor, Littlehampton Book Services on 01903 721596
For a catalogue of these and our other titles please ring Regina Schinner on 01453 731114